FATAL
CONCEIT

Richard W. Dortch

New Leaf Press

First printing: July 1993
Second printing: April 1994

Library of Congress Catalog Number: 92-63373
ISBN: 0-89221-245-4

Note: Some names have been changed to protect the identity and privacy of those involved.

Acknowledgments

Without my family, I could not have written *Fatal Conceit.*

Before I had completed my previous book, *Integrity: How I Lost It and My Journey Back,* I told my publishers, the late Clifford Dudley and his son Tim, what was burning inside me. I was made to know that I had to write *Fatal Conceit.* I had more than a story to tell. *Integrity* was about what happened at PTL. This book tells the story of why it happened.

The late Cliff Dudley and his wife Harriett, their son Tim and daughter Becky, continue the great tradition of excellence in publishing by New Leaf Press. Cliff was a friend who pushed me on to write, to listen to my heart, and to remember promptings from my Heavenly Father. I am a debtor to these friends, whose kindness to me will always be remembered.

Judy Lewis and everyone at New Leaf Press have offered their help. It is deeply appreciated.

When I began this project, Jeff Dunn helped me. In addition, my friend, Dan Johnson, who is like a brother to me, encouraged me to write what was on my heart.

Dr. Ray Meaders guided me when I needed insight.

Mark and Wanda Burgund are gifts of God to my family and to me. Wanda is a professional counselor who helped me cut through the rhetoric to get to the point.

During this year of preparation and writing, my bishop, Dr. Gordon Matheny, was a friend that I called upon in times of need.

Two men that I labor with at Life Challenge, Peter Waldron and Jim Capo, were sounding boards and helped me carry the load.

My editor, Val Cindric, and marketing consultant, Joyce Hart, have been guiding hands in the birth of this labor of love. Our publicist, Jacqueline Cromartie, is simply the best in the business.

Many friends and colleagues gave me the encouragement to press on.

My sweetheart, my wife, my friend, Mildred has lived through this process with me, and suffered, I am sure, through my failures. I am eternally grateful for her standing by my side and for giving me the courage to keep going.

The chairman of our board of Life Challenge, Dr. Arthur Parsons and his wife, Usteena, have been a constant source of strength to Mildred and me. His wisdom and guidance have been invaluable. Other than my family, he had the most to do with my restoration. He really cared about us and did something about it. His life of humility has been a constant source of light in the dark corners of my life. He ministered to me greatly while I was writing this book. I continue to submit myself to his leadership.

Two of my attorneys continue to counsel me in matters related to the writing of this book, in my personal life, and in the work of Life Challenge. Mr. Mark Calloway of Charlotte, North Carolina and Mr. George Tragos of Clearwater, Florida, attorneys at law, are examples of what this book is about. They are two who walk wisely and humbly.

In the writing of this book our daughter Deanna and her

family, and our son Rich and his family, were constant reminders to us of God's faithfulness. They had insight and help for me as only our children can provide. I value their love and judgment.

Dedication

I lovingly dedicate this book to the memory of my pastor, my bishop, my friend.

The Rev. Dr. Thomas F. Zimmerman

Whose life of achievement and excellence understood the dangers of fatal conceit.

He was a religious statesman of great power. He used it nobly, wisely, and humbly. His wife, Elizabeth, shares our esteem. He is now in that place that is *"far better."*

CONTENTS

Preface

Within these pages, you will learn what it is like to let power and pride destroy your life. I know because I've been there and back. It is a grievous and hurtful process, and even today, I am still learning from my mistakes.

I am a composite of all that I have studied, experienced, read, and assimilated. In writing this book I have been helped by many people. They gave me ideas, materials, and experiences from their own lives. For several years I have read, searched, and obtained as much as I could acquire about the subjects that we will discuss.

Much of what I have studied has become such a part of me that I really can't tell what ideas and thoughts originated with me. No attempt has been made to take credit for anything. Whatever I have put into this book, from any source, all of us want to lay it at our Master's feet.

I am very hopeful that as you read this book, you will read it in the same spirit in which it was written. This is not a book for weaker souls. It is intense. I am deeply burdened, fearful of what we are becoming. I have seen up close, first hand, the results of fatal conceit. In our society it is affecting many more of us than we want to admit.

I sincerely pray that as the light shines in the dark

corners of our lives, we will all have a wonderful illumination. I desperately want to be a better person, and I hope that will happen to you because of what this book is bringing to light. It is the truth that sets all of us free.

The royalties of this book are being given to Life Challenge, a non-profit agency that assists professionals who are going through a crisis in their lives. Often they are people who have lost everything. Some have forfeited their integrity and their reputations; others are experiencing financial and legal problems. A few have even lost their freedom. All, however, come seeking our help.

Because I have walked through this process myself, I know how much it helps to have someone walk with you through the pain. We have a vision to make Life Challenge a caring place of refuge for people who need love and forgiveness in their time of crisis. It is happening.

Introduction

Shortly after I was released from prison, I talked to my dear friend, Steve Strang, publisher of *Charisma* magazine and Creation House books. I thanked him for his kindness as a brother to care about what had happened in my life.

"I really learned something from what you went through," Steve told me.

I was taken aback.

"You learned something from my failure?" I asked.

"Yes, I learned if it can happen to you, it can happen to anybody."

That's why I am writing this for you and to you. We often read an article or a book, and immediately think of all the people we know who "really need to hear this."

I am speaking to you in this treatise. It is you that I have in my mind and heart as I write this book.

Why? Because I am convinced that our most basic problem as human beings is pride and lust for power. I believe it is your problem, and I know it is mine. It is seductive, and it comes to us in subtle ways. It is the fatal conceit. I was even considering calling the book "Power — How I Lost It and Why I Don't Want It Back."

There are many church-going "Christians" who believe they are the "blue-bloods" among us. They are elitists, the aristocracy of Christendom. Among them are people who claim to believe the "full gospel." In business, they say they are the biggest and the best. In politics, the claim is heralded that they will be the best man for the office. In education, it is said, "We train the 'best' students." Is that conceit and is it fatal?

But they are not the exceptions. You can find people with the same attitude at home, in the work place, and in other parts of our lives. Are these the people who believe they must control others and events? Is this pride and conceit? Often these are people who are the last to see themselves as they are.

The worst sort of pride is spiritual pride. Great claims are made by Evangelicals, Charismatics, and classic Pentecostals. They leave the impression sometimes that they are a little better, more spiritual, have more of God and a fuller revelation of the Bible than others. Do the facts substantiate such a claim? Is there evidence of that among us? Are they really better than the rest of us? What they do have many times is more arrogance, pride, and conceit.

It is fatal, it is and will be our downfall unless there is genuine repentance and a breaking of self. We are not better than anyone else, so perhaps we should admit the truth and remember that there are no works of righteousness of which we should boast.

I have never met or known a person who really believed and practiced the "full gospel." I have heard and seen many who have claimed to, but they do not show it. They accept certain portions of Scripture that give them a reason for being — but *full* gospel? Is that really what we mean? Why do we want to be better, bigger, and more full?

When it is necessary to announce how good, spiritual, and *full* we are, it leaves much to be desired. People know what we are, and our lives speak for themselves.

Adam did not commit the first sin recorded in Scripture; Lucifer did. He wanted to be equal with God, and there is some of that in all of us. We bow most often at the altar of the mirror. It is pride in its ugliest form.

Our quest for power and how we have abused it is — for each of us — a fatal conceit.

What went wrong at PTL? What brought down men like Ivan Boesky, Jimmy Swaggart, Richard Nixon, Michael Milkin, Leona Helmsley, Richard Dortch? Where did we all go wrong? I can tell you. We thought we were above it all!

But they are just the tip of the iceberg — just the skin of the rotten apple fermenting from within.

In the past five years, every area of government, education, business, and the church has been touched by the time bomb ticking within all of us — this fatal conceit. What we've seen and what continues to be revealed is merely a prelude to what is to come.

Next time it won't be only the people on the fringe. Instead, those at the center of our highest and most respected institutions of government, education, and the church will be exposed. It is happening now, but we have yet to see the full impact.

Is our nation destroying itself from within? Have we entered a world of fatal conceit? Will it affect us all?

How can we identify our situation and circumstance? Will our conceit permit us to honestly look at ourselves? The quest for power goes on. It is conceit, and it is fatal.

Walk with me now on a journey beyond the looking glass and into the deepest recesses of our hearts.

1

The Majesty of the Moment

In fear of tragedy, we worship power.
In fear of suffering, we worship security.
In fear of failure, we worship success.
During the rising splendor of our thousand
prosperous years, we had grown cruel, practical,
and sterile. We did win the whole world. We did
lose our own souls.

Robert Raynolds

The route we took that Sunday morning through down-town Dallas seemed familiar. Something important had happened here. Something tragic.

Then I recognized the route as the same one taken by the driver of John F. Kennedy's car after the president had been shot in November 1963. Kennedy's car had sped along this very road; his lifeless body clutched in the arms of his horrified wife.

As I reflected on the senseless death of this leader, it seemed as if I, too, was on the verge of death.

In the past five years, my life had been uprooted from its stable and secure position as a leader in my denomination. Then as the executive director of PTL Ministries, I appeared with Jim Bakker on the daily television program. I had pleaded guilty to charges of wire and mail fraud in connection with offering lifetime partnerships at a resort complex on the grounds of PTL's Heritage USA in Charlotte, North Carolina. Sentenced to eight years at Eglin Federal Prison Camp, I served twenty-one months and eight days.

I lost almost everything. My money went to cover legal fees. My denomination revoked my credentials. People whom I thought were my friends no longer phoned or wrote.

Truly, I thought that Sunday morning in Dallas, *many have given me up for dead.*

A few months before, I had taken a similar journey on a Sunday morning, driving from my home in Tampa, Florida to the Carpenter's Home Church in Lakeland, a large church pastored by my dear friends, Karl and Joyce Strader. There I publicly confessed my sins and asked Pastor Strader's congregation to forgive me for hurting them. They were overwhelming in their gracious response.

This Sunday morning I was on my way to face some of the most respected and well-known men and women in Christendom.

Don George, pastor of Calvary Temple in the Dallas/Ft. Worth metroplex, had invited me to speak to his congregation and guests. Constantly on my mind was the thought that the Christian Booksellers Association's annual convention was being held in Dallas at the same time.

I knew Pastor George very well. He had been a true friend down through the years to my wife and me. His congregation had always received us warmly in the past. I had spoken at Calvary Temple many times before they built their beautiful, mammoth cathedral and later participated in the dedication of the completed facility. Yet, I was now filled with fear at the thought of speaking there, especially before many nationally known ministers, businessmen, authors, singers, and television personalities who would be in the service.

Anxiety had gripped me almost every day for the past two months whenever I thought about my scheduled engagement at Calvary. I knew this was not going to be just an encounter with a congregation or even well-known ministers and celebrities.

This was going to be an encounter with me. An encounter I had to face sooner or later.

Unfinished Business

As we neared the church, I wondered, *Would there be the crowd they were expecting?* Perhaps only the local congregation would know I was coming. But as we came to the freeway exit for the church, a giant marquee loomed ahead of us, announcing Richard Dortch as that morning's guest speaker. Most of the convention attendees would surely have seen the sign on their way in from the airport. There was no hope of escape now.

Immediately I knew what I had to do. I was "made to know" — this is the way I describe God's promptings to me — that I must confess my sins and ask forgiveness, apologizing to the people in the church that morning for the hurt and reproach I had brought on the gospel. I knew that was the right thing to do, and with God's grace I could do it.

The members and Pastor George lovingly greeted Mildred and me as we made our way into the church. After a few choruses and the opening prayer, I stood to my feet and, with trembling knees and breaking heart, approached the pulpit.

"Pastor George," I began, my voice barely above a whisper, "thank you for your kind introduction, but please stay here at the pulpit with me. There is some unfinished business I need to do before I speak."

Silence filled the cathedral. I could sense the audience waiting for my next word.

"This church," I continued, "has been a friend to Mildred and me for many years. I hurt you, Pastor. I brought shame to my friends, this church, and the body of Christ. I brought reproach to you as a person and to this group of people, and for this I am very sorry. I ask each of you to forgive me, and I plead with this congregation to forgive me. I know God has forgiven me, but now I need to ask you to forgive me because I so regret the pain I brought into your lives."

As I ceased talking, I felt as if time itself had stopped. The audience appeared stunned by my confession. All the respected people I had expected to be there were seated throughout the church that morning. Yet, through God's grace, I faced my sins and publicly confessed the things I had done wrong.

I waited for what seemed like an eternity, then I heard a sob, and then another. Someone stood and began to weep. Then I felt the warm arm of Pastor George around me. With tears, he hugged me intensely, whispering, "you are forgiven." At that moment I was lost in a world of love.

When I regained my composure, the congregation was standing, some applauding, some weeping. I looked at them through my tears, wondering what had just happened and what would happen next.

After a few minutes, the people quieted down, and Pastor George stepped to the microphone. "Richard Dortch," he said, looking directly into my eyes, "you are forgiven. We want you to know the peace we have all found. Never again to this congregation need you say anything about the past. We forgive you, just as we have been forgiven. You are loved."

The majesty of the moment was overwhelming. Not

the majesty of my being center stage, or in front of many of the mighty men and women of faith I knew and respected. The majesty of that moment came from within. It came as I asked forgiveness for my sins.

Confronting Myself

After my confession before the believers of Calvary Church, I determined that, if I must go before every congregation that invites me to speak and confess my failure, I would do it.

Although confessing my sin and asking and receiving forgiveness brought great healing to my heart and mind, I knew the process was not complete. I needed to do more than confess to others; I needed to confront myself. I knew I had to search my soul to discover the reasons for my transgressions and downfall.

After many months of self-examination and near total despair, I identified the root of my sin: I had violated the power entrusted to me by God and by my brothers and sisters in the faith. I had tried to seize some of God's glory, and He would have none of it.

God shares His glory with no one, but I had wanted some attention. I had wanted acclamation. I had wanted power to do with as I pleased. I got all of that along with a good dose of chastisement and humiliation.

From the time I stepped down as superintendent of my church denomination in the state of Illinois to take the position with the PTL ministry until the day I was released from prison, more than five years had passed. During that time I constantly faced the issue of how the violation of power had eroded the integrity I had spent a lifetime building.

In my heart, however, I knew my tenure at PTL was not the first time in my life I had longed for power.

After our family returned from the mission field, where I had helped start a ministerial training center for French speaking people in Europe, I became pastor of a prominent church in Illinois. Not long after that, I was elected as an overseer of about twenty-five churches in our denomination in the metropolitan St. Louis area. While remaining a pastor, this gave me a seat on the state board of our denomination in Illinois. It all happened so quickly.

I had served on the mission field in a lowly, apparently non-recognizable role. Then, within months of coming back to the United States, I found myself, as a young pastor, sitting on a prestigious board for our denomination.

The Tail Wagging the Dog

The leader of my denomination in Illinois at the time was Dr. E.M. Clark, an upright, loving, and brilliant man. Dr. Clark's main concern was for the welfare of the pastors and the aggressive building of the kingdom of God.

It was at a board meeting with Dr. Clark that I began to see my true nature. The condition of my heart at that time caused me to think more of myself than I should and to want power that was not meant for me.

During the meeting, Dr. Clark outlined a plan for pastors and churches — a plan calling for sacrifice and commitment. I saw his plan as one that would detract from me and my efforts.

In my foolishness I spoke up and said, "Well, it seems to me, in this organization, the tail is wagging the dog."

This beloved leader looked at me, obviously stunned at such a remark. But in my cockiness and lust for power, I could only think of myself, and it didn't register fully as to what I had done.

The next evening, when I went to my room to spend quiet time with the Lord, I was in for a rude awakening. After reading the Scripture and meditating, I paused to hear what the Lord would say to me. Rather than hearing the usual comforting tone of God, I sensed a voice within saying, "It seems to me the tail is wagging the dog."

I quickly jumped in bed, pulled the sheets over me, and asked the Lord to help me sleep. I didn't want to deal with what I was hearing in my heart.

In the morning, I again tried to maintain my devotional life, telling the Lord how much I wanted His presence that day. The response I heard was, "It seems to me the tail is wagging the dog."

This continued for the next several days — long enough for me to realize that His words were not going to change until I changed. Finally, I came face to face with myself and asked, *What should I do to make this right?*

I was made to know in plain non-religious terms, "You shall get in your little red car, take a journey of 50 miles, find Dr. Clark, and admit you are a cocky, mean-spirited jerk. You will confess what a nasty person you were to say such a thing in that board meeting."

My response to the voice within me was, "Lord, I'd just as soon not do this." After placating myself for a period of time, I finally faced the reality of what I had to do.

I cautiously phoned our esteemed bishop and asked if he would be in his office that day, hoping he had other plans. "Yes," he replied, "I will be in all afternoon." Somehow I knew he would.

Upon arrival and being greeted by our leader, I stalled by asking, "How's Mrs. Clark? I hope your grandchildren are all doing well."

Then a voice within me, made me to know, "Admit your evil ways."

Finally I stopped and said, "Brother Clark, do you remember several weeks ago at our meeting when I made a comment about the tail wagging the dog? Do you remember that?" I was hoping, with great longing, that he had forgotten.

He stared at me for a moment, searching into my eyes and soul. Then he nodded his head in the affirmative, "Yes, I remember it very well."

The time had come. I looked at him and humbly said, "Brother Clark, I am a misguided, wretched soul. I have been cocky and stuck on myself, and I have acted terribly. Could you find it in your heart to forgive me? I said something I never should have said. I am here today to ask for your forgiveness."

He stood up from his seat, came around the desk, and embraced me. "You were forgiven before you said anything," he replied.

My Desire

All through my life and ministry, I have known a part of my nature is to desire power, make a name for myself, to gather attention around me, to have my own way. Sometimes I have conquered this desire; sometimes it has conquered me. I'm deeply troubled by it because I know I am never more like the enemy of our souls than when I grab for power.

I don't want to be like our common enemy; I want to be like my Master.

While I know God's power of forgiveness is greater than my power of selfishness, I have set out to understand the mysterious attraction of power and its seduction. I want to recognize its characteristics and put myself on guard against its subtle attempts to destroy my life and the lives of others.

2

The Faces of Power

Isolation from reality is inseparable from the exercise of power.

George Reedy

"I'm J. Paul Getty, and E.F. Hutton is my broker."

For nearly a century this respected brokerage house served thousands of clients — many of them among the rich and famous — like the man in their commercial, J. Paul Getty.

But whatever happened to, "When E.F. Hutton talks . . . people listen"?

The answer is simple.

Bob Fomon served twenty-five years as CEO of E.F. Hutton and led the company to spectacular growth, but he "spent his career leasing private jets, padding the payroll with cronies, and housing pets in company apartments."

According to Mark Stevens in his book, *Sudden Death: The Rise and Fall of E.F. Hutton,*[1] the thirty-story glass and pink granite corporate palace of E.F. Hutton once located on West 52nd Street in New York City housed "nine private dining rooms with state-of-the-art kitchen facilities, a health club, a private art collection, toilets fit for kings."

A former associate recalled, "Bob couched his extravagance in the idea that the industry was moving uptown. . . . But Fomon simply wanted a monument, a permanent symbol of the man who'd built it."

What drives a person to crave the accolades of his generation and sell his soul for wealth and fame? The seeds were sown early in Bob Fomon's life.

After Fomon's mother died when he was four, he was raised by an aunt in Appleton, Wisconsin. Estranged from his father, a physician, young Bob grew up a rebel with a not-so-subtle streak of arrogance. He pursued a career in finance in California where he fell in love with wealth and the power it brings. The rest of his life was spent cultivating the rich and famous and accumulating material possessions.

Bob Fomon's philosophy was summed up in an interview with *Money* magazine in 1986: "Because of so many years of experience, I may have more wisdom than some other people, and the fact that I may have the power to out vote others is a good feeling. Most people will not admit that there is a great satisfaction and pleasure in power."

His considerable skills enhanced the fortunes of E.F. Hutton, but his avarice, greed, and lust spelled its ruin. "All of this grotesque indulgence was being squandered at a time when Hutton needed to cut back," Mark Stevens writes.

The seeds of collapse — ostentation, extravagant facilities, lavish lifestyles, and enormous debt — grew out of control like a giant beanstalk waiting to be felled.

"The autumn of 1987," Stevens writes, "shortly after the October crash, obliterated any hopes for its survival. E.F. Hutton became history, sold at a fire-sale price to Shearson-Lehman."

Still, I miss the commercial, "When E.F. Hutton talks . . . people listen."

What Is Power?

No one knows better than I the price that fatal conceit demands. I served nearly a year and a half of my life in a federal prison because I violated the power entrusted to me at PTL. Over the years, I have observed others who have misused their positions of authority. It is a sad scenario played out in homes, businesses, education, governments, churches, schools, and ministries daily.

Before we can overcome the abuse of power, we must have a clear understanding of what power is.

The dictionary defines power as "the ability to control others; to act with authority; sway and influence."

That definition of power describes many honest, hardworking people who daily act with authority, sway, and influence. Employers try to influence their employees to do their best. Teachers exercise discipline over their pupils in order to prevent chaos in the classroom. Police officers use authority and force within the limits of the law. These are examples of power used properly and effectively.

Power denotes the inherent ability or the admitted right to rule and govern others — to determine what others will and will not do.

Theologians say power is the capability of one person to produce intended results in others, voluntarily or involuntarily.

Wesley Pippert, a respected journalist and White House correspondent who observes the power game firsthand in Washington, DC, writes: "Power is the ability to shape and influence people and/or events."[2]

Who Wields Power?

We mistakenly assume that power rests only with the elite. But that's not true. Each of us has power in many areas of our lives. We have sway over a circle of people — our family, our close friends, neighbors, people in government, our business associates, and those in our Sunday school class or committees at church. We exercise influence when we buy one brand of bread over another at the grocery store.

Leadership is influence, and everyone influences at least three people. How we use that influence reveals the motive of our hearts.

Wesley Pippert writes,

> Since all of us can wield power through our unique abilities, all of us are subject to the temptation of abusing power. Fathers abuse children, and husbands and wives will abuse their spouse, whether it is verbal or physical abuse. Some exercise power with the information and knowledge they possess. Others have power through their ability to speak persuasively.[3]

To one person visibility is power; others equate physical strength and endurance as power. Power is cloaked in many costumes. Underneath, however, power's motivating force is self-centeredness.

Knowledge, visibility, speech, seniority, information, trust, self-confidence, access to important people, the ability to delay or obstruct, a title or social status — these are the tools of power-seekers.

We often think only those in prominent positions — politicians, entertainers, preachers, teachers — have power. Power, however, does not always present itself in bright lights and big headlines. Like the tiny rock used to kill the giant Goliath, power often enters our lives in small, subtle ways.

Even an unknown can invoke a power play. Some people will say, "I'm a nobody. No one listens to what I say." That can be a ploy to arouse sympathy or pity in others. When it works, the seemingly weak obtain control. Some people use illness or personal problems to maintain their supremacy, doing whatever is necessary to be in power.

We've all heard — or repeated to ourselves — statements of power that reveal our true nature:

"If I leave this church or this business, it will fall apart."

"Do people really understand what a good job I am doing?"

"I deserve a bigger office."

"Why should I have to do this job? It's beneath a person of my position."

"Is this the best spot for me to stand in the choir?"

Where is the power game played? It's played in every corner of life, including politics, business, the home, the church, ministries, government, relationships, the media. It especially raises its ugly head in situations where the handling of money is involved.

Someone defined the golden rule principle as: "Those who have the gold rule."

The advantages of power are difficult to resist, and few of us refuse them. Author Sheryl Forbes describes power as "a god, and a heady, intoxicating one." Success is its creed.

We've all played the power game where presenting a successful image becomes an acquired skill. We wear the right clothes; repeat the politically correct phrases; and do what we know will work to maintain a "proper image." Success takes precedence over everything else in our lives, and pride sets itself up on the throne of our hearts.

Who Has Power?

I had power.

Some of us in high profile ministries failed to practice what we preached, and, as a result, brought shame and hurt to many.

I know now what led to our downfall. It was all about power, being big, having the most supporters, and maintaining an expensive lifestyle. Our actions brought reproach on all that is sacred.

Today the public lists religious media personalities at

the bottom of honored professions. The skepticism is understandable, and, sadly, we brought most of it upon ourselves. As a result, our most treasured institutions have all borne the hit!

Unfortunately, the American people appear to have learned little from the recent scandals unearthed in business, government, the media, education, and the church; the fraud and failure of the savings and loan institutions; the greed and swindling of bank officers; the bad checks written by members of Congress; the falsified documents and the fraudulent acceptance of government funds by universities and colleges; and ministries that misled their supporters.

One thing we *have* learned is that successful liars and manipulators can be found in the highest offices of the land and that their professions take many forms. It goes with the territory. Those with less visible positions in society also find ways to scratch and claw their way to the top of the heap — whether it's the coach of their son's soccer team or chairman of the banquet committee.

How about you? Are you in some position of power that affords you the opportunity to lord it over others? Do you use your authority in negative ways to control your children, your spouse, the PTA mothers, your subordinates at work, the Sunday school class, or the check-out clerks at the grocery store?

No one is exempt. We're all tempted — either regularly or occasionally.

The Slow Cooker

While I was in prison, the stress and emotional turmoil of the experience often caused the symptoms of my intestinal disease to erupt.

One night as I sat on my cot, holding my side in agony from the pain, I said out loud in my distress, "I hurt so bad."

An inmate from the next row of beds in the dormitory walked over, sat down beside me, and put his hand on my shoulder. "Richard, maybe I can offer some help," he said. I looked up at my friend who had been an army general and a prominent physician before being sent to prison.

"Thanks, Dr. Evans," I replied. "But it's my Crohn's disease acting up."

"I know," he said. "I taught medical school at Columbia University in New York with Dr. Crohn. I knew him well. Let me see if there's something I can do to relieve the pain."

For a moment, I just stared at him, wondering how in the world a successful physician and medical school professor had ended up in prison. Of course, I didn't ask; that's an unwritten law of prison life. But I still couldn't imagine what crime this kind, caring doctor had committed. But what right did I have to ask? I was in prison myself.

In fact, I don't believe any of the men — among them judges, government agents, bankers, lawyers, doctors, ministers, custom agents, police, politicians — serving time in Eglin prison got up one morning and said, "Today's the day I'm going to be a crook." It doesn't happen that way. Slowly over time, in their grab for power and money, they compromised their values and made fatal mistakes.

Like the frog being slowly boiled in water, they didn't realize the danger until the soup got too hot and it was too late to escape.

Familiar Faces

Every week I looked forward to a time of Bible study with the other inmates in the prison. This was not just jail house religion, however. These men, many of whom had served in places of leadership, sincerely wanted to take a look at their lives and their relationship with God. Over and over again, we grappled with the question that haunted all of us: How did we get here?

One day during that Bible study, a former successful stockbroker said, "I went wrong when I began to ascend to power in my company."

On another occasion, a doctor who had been convicted of fraud looked at me and said, "I sold out when I considered myself to be invincible. The Medicare and Medicaid funds are so easy to get, I figured, why not take several hundred thousands of dollars? Who would ever know?"

One evening, I sat for hours and listened to a man who had formerly been a secret service agent for President Reagan. He, too, told where he had gone wrong. He began to believe he was above it all because of his position with the government. He thought he could take a boat trip and be part of illegal drug operations without any consequences. The deception of power had deluded him, and he fell headlong into fatal conceit.

My perception of the power trap grew as I heard others talk about the experiences that had started them down the road to prison.

An evangelist friend said to me, "I thought I could take money that was not mine and pay it back. The scary thing is I actually believed that. I didn't know how I could ever pay the money back. But my desire for the good life was so great I couldn't see that I was breaking the rules."

The former pastor of a large metropolitan church — a man who had been honored by the president of the United States — bared his soul to me one day. "I used my credit cards when I knew I shouldn't have," he said, "and I knew in the back of my mind that my spending could cause big problems down the road. Still, I did nothing about it. I was so intoxicated with my vision that I lost sight of who I was and what I was doing. For a while I didn't even care."

These men were highly educated — some with doctoral degrees; they had well-paying jobs, outstanding reputations, and status in their communities. But they had all played the power game and lost.

The Big Lie

What does the power that destroys look like?

Think of Adam and Eve in the Garden. Given every pleasure, every delight, everything necessary for a good life, they still wanted more. They grasped and grabbed in a headlong rush to be like God — to know good and evil.

The sin of the Garden of Eden was the sin of power. Adam and Eve wanted to be more, to have more, to know more than is right. Not content to be creatures, they wanted to be gods.

Adam and Eve, like so many of their descendants after them, swallowed, what I call, "The Big Lie."

The serpent deceived Eve into thinking that by disobeying God — by taking authority that was not hers — she would actually be pleasing God. This is the root of all of our violations of power: assuming we know better than our Maker what is best for us.

God is the ultimate source of all power; so when we violate power given us, we act in disobedience to Him.

Are you — like Adam and Eve — trying to be equal with God?

[1]Mark Stevens, *Sudden Death: The Rise and Fall of E.F. Hutton* (New York, NY: New American Library, 1989).
[2]Wesley Pippert, *The Hand of the Mighty: Right and Wrong Uses of Our Power* (Grand Rapids, MI: Baker Book House/Revell, 1991).
[3]Ibid.

3

Misplaced Power

*Power destroys relationships. Climb, push,
and shove is the language of power.*

Richard Foster

Three o'clock one Friday afternoon, I was walking
across the prison compound at Eglin Federal Prison when I
heard my name blasted over the loudspeaker.

"Richard Dortch! Come to the control room!"

Such an announcement always called for a quick
response.

When I arrived, Mrs. Franks, the officer in charge,
commanded, "Go to your dormitory immediately and get
your things. On Monday morning, you will be leaving on a
Federal Writ."

I knew that meant I was supposed to return to Charlotte,
North Carolina to testify in a case. But my attorney had not
informed me of this decision, so I supposed the officer must
be mistaken.

"I don't think I'll be going back to Charlotte yet," I
responded.

An inmate should never contradict an officer but, because I had only been in prison a short while, I didn't know any better.

With a stern look, she replied harshly, "You do what you're told to do!"

I politely asked, "Could we call my lawyer?" which in most circumstances would be permitted. It wasn't her authority I was questioning, but the manner in which she exercised that authority by refusing to listen to me.

"No!" she commanded. "Go get your things."

As I left the control room, all I could think about was the supposed transfer. When a federal inmate leaves the prison on a federal writ, he is taken by bus, with shackled feet and hands, to a center and transferred to another bus. The inmates refer to this procedure as "diesel therapy." If, however, the court destination is some distance away, the prisoner travels via a Bureau of Prisons airplane, commonly called "Con Air."

En route the prisoner is usually lodged overnight in a county jail. That's what every inmate fears most. The stories I had heard about such incarcerations made my hair stand on end. To make matters worse, I was concerned about my health because the officer told me I would not be able to take my medication with me. "Absolutely nothing!" she had said.

Her lack of compassion and common decency left me dazed and in shock.

Deeply troubled, I went back to the modular cube where I slept. Because of the lateness of the hour, the counselor in my dormitory had already gone home for the evening. Later I got to a phone where I was able to call my lawyer.

He quickly informed me, "Don't worry about it. I've talked to the prosecutor, and you won't be going to Charlotte at this time."

I had been instructed by Mrs. Franks, "Monday morning I will call you in, and when I do, bring the clothes that you've used on the weekend and anything else you haven't already turned in."

Just after entering Eglin as an inmate, I had been told by a pastor friend that Mrs. Franks was a wonderful Christian woman who worked at the prison. Long before the encounter in the control room, I had asked another inmate if he knew her. To my shock, he and a group of inmates who heard my question had laughed and said, "Oh, you mean that 'Christian' officer!"

At eight o'clock Monday morning, she called for me. I responded and went to control, hoping that the pastor's assessment had been more accurate than the inmates'.

When she saw me she asked, "Where are your things, the things you've worn on the weekend?"

I replied, "Well, I talked to my lawyer, and he told me that the marshals aren't coming."

I could see the heat rising in her face. "I'm not interested in your story," she shouted. "Go get your things and do it now and don't question what I ask you to do!"

I began to say, "Well, you know . . ." She cut me off.

I just stood there and began to cry.

It wasn't what she was saying that bothered me; it was the officious, belligerent attitude that she displayed. This was not an official carrying out her orders; she was trying to send a message about her authority.

I hastened back to the dormitory and talked with my counselor, whom I respected and who always acted in a professional manner with no strings attached. For the most part, I found those employed by the Bureau of Prisons to be competent and capable. In fact, I bear no ill will toward anyone I met during that experience.

I explained the situation to him, "The officer in control has told me that I'm to get my things and go out on a federal writ."

He replied, "I've talked to the prosecutor and to your

attorney, and you are not going."

I said, "Well she's insisting that I bring my things."

He told me, "You simply go back and tell her that you are not going to be signed out."

I returned to the control office and told the officer what my counselor had said. She flew into a rage, "What do you think you're doing by going over my head?"

Taken aback, I responded, "I thought that was what a counselor was for — to go to with any problems."

In a very abrasive way, she ordered me out of the control area and said threateningly, "I'll deal with this."

For days, I lived in absolute fear, wondering what form her retribution would take. Those were some of my most frightful and anxious moments in prison.

Intoxicated With Power

After that incident, I began to think about power and what it does to people. I knew that people in authority had to have power over others in order to do their jobs and accomplish their purposes. If, in order to hold their position, however, they have to change their personality, take leave of their humanity, and forfeit their supposed Christianity, something is wrong.

People who are intoxicated with power have a mind set only on their own personal agenda. Often these people have unresolved issues in their own lives, but they refuse to deal with them. It's often these unresolved sins or problems, however, that drive them to be in positions of power over others.

It's the case of the man who has been unfaithful to his wife, the father whose child has disappointed him, the politician who wants a higher office and isn't elected. When a person living in sin or with deep hurts and insecurities arrives at a place of power, his objectivity is clouded. Instead of dealing rationally with issues that confront him, he is always on the attack. With every encounter, he is actually dealing vicariously with his own problem.

The office worker who commits a minor infraction is nailed to the wall, not because of his misdeed, but because of the boss's own unresolved sin or insecurity. In meting out the discipline, he seeks to appease his own conscience or vent his suppressed anger over the unresolved situation in his life.

I recall a minister whose daughter went through a divorce. He was concerned because he felt that her broken marriage could reflect on his ministry. The minister's perceived embarrassment over the situation took precedence over his relationship with his daughter, and he alienated himself from her. The more concerned he was about his position, the more distance he put between them. His lust for power and future position meant more to him than his own child who was hurting deeply.

As a result, almost everyone who came into contact with this man found him to be mean spirited, judgmental, and abrasive. His behavior resulted, not from what others had done but because of his own personal problems. Instead of acting properly as an authority figure, he misused power and created difficulties for his daughter, and, ultimately, for his own ministry.

Richard Foster, writing in *Money, Sex, and Power* says, "If money hits us in the pocketbook, and sex hits us in the bedroom, power hits us in our relationships."[1]

Power can destroy or create. The power that destroys creates ascendancy. It demands total control and destroys relationships. As a result, it destroys trust and meaningful dialogue between people.

At the Top

Through the crisis agency of Life Challenge, we counsel those whose lives have been devastated by the fatal conceit of power.

One day a young man came to me, broken in spirit and

filled with remorse. His story, however, is not unusual.

When Kurt got out of college, serving God and mankind was his highest goal. A good husband, father, businessman, and civic leader, he had everything going for him. Everyone noticed his superb leadership skills, and soon his friends in the community asked him to run for the office of county commissioner.

His Christian commitment, his reputation of honesty, and his family values got Kurt elected. In spite of the heavy workload of the new position, he continued to make time for his wife and family.

Before long, his excellent work as a county commissioner brought his name and reputation before the political party officials. When the position of state senator from his district came open, he was urged to run for the office. His wife, Carol, in discussing the matter with him said, "Be sure that this is what you should do." She could sense that Kurt was yielding to a pull that went beyond his desire to serve. It was more than service that he wanted; it was the position of power.

After his election as a state senator, his life changed dramatically. He was now at the top; he had what he wanted. At the capital, he had people to meet and appearances to make. His life became his job. He now belonged to the public, leaving little or no time for his family. The once long discussions that had meant so much to Carol became fewer and farther between.

When Carol frequently mentioned church or family to Kurt, her cautions went unheeded, especially if she pushed too hard. "Maybe you need to spend more time with me and the kids," she would remind him. Her warnings, however, fell on deaf ears, and the young couple began to pull apart.

As position and power consumed him, greed got a foothold in Kurt's heart. Everyone could see it but him. It wasn't long before he had to be with "his people" to accomplish his goals.

Carol felt he no longer needed her. Her feelings were confirmed when she learned he had been unfaithful. With their marriage in a shambles, Carol and Kurt separated, leaving their children's lives deeply bruised.

After his second term, the reputation that had put him in office was no longer recognizable by his constituency. He lost the election.

The power that had so tempted him and brought him to the top had vanished along with the family he had loved the most. He had fixed his sights on the temporary thrill of the moment, and, as a result, the permanent was lost.

At this tragic point in his life, he couldn't find his way back. He came to Life Challenge for help.

The Price of Power

Paul Tournier writes, "Power is the greatest obstacle in the way of dialogue. We pay dearly for our power."

We see the evidence of lost dialogue everywhere: between husband and wife, between parent and child, and between employer and employee.

Power's ability to destroy human relationships is written across the face of humanity.

In a chapter entitled "The Impotence of Power" in his book *Money, Sex, and Power,* Richard Foster writes,

> Power cannot command affection, and the people loved David. Saul was powerless to control the hearts of the people so he turned in rage against David. He would rather have murdered than to have allowed power to slip through his fingers. Power destroys relationships. Climb, push, and shove is the language of power.[2]

What makes us want to rule over people? To be the boss, the top dog. Is there some warped worm growing inside us?

"Amazing, isn't it," Richard Foster writes, "grownup people deeply exercised over who is at the top of the heap."

In his book, *The Pursuit of God*, A.W. Tozer describes the real problem facing us as human beings:

> All of our heartaches, and a great many of our physical ills spring directly out of our sins. Pride, arrogance, resentfulness, evil imaginings, malice, greed: these are the sources of more human pain than all the diseases that ever afflicted mortal flesh.[3]

Lee Atwater, a brilliant architect of Republican victories who was chairman of the Republican party and headed Bush's successful campaign for the presidency, achieved success in the political arena by destroying the reputation of his opponents. At the height of wealth, fame, and power, Lee Atwater was struck down by a brain tumor that left him a human wreck. In the midst of this personal tragedy, however, he came to Jesus Christ and was gloriously converted. Listen to his words, as written in *Life* magazine:

> The eighties were about acquiring — acquiring of wealth, the acquisition of wealth, power, prestige. I know. I acquired more wealth, power, and prestige than most. But you can acquire all you want and still feel empty. What power wouldn't I trade for a little more time with my family. What price wouldn't I pay for an evening with my friends. It took a deadly illness to put me eye to eye with that truth, but it is a truth that the country, caught up in its ruthless ambitions and moral decay, can learn on my dime. I don't know who will lead us through the nineties, but they must be made to speak to this spiritual vacuum at the heart of American society, this tumor of the soul.

What is this tumor on the soul of man?

It's the false belief that we don't need God. That we can do it ourselves without Him.

Most of us, however, deny that this is our problem. We just don't get it.

To deny the fact, however, leaves us in a vulnerable place. We set ourselves up for failure when we do refuse to see our need for humility and continue in our overt acts of arrogance.

Such pride is not just the problem of prominent, high profile people. This is not an issue reserved for politicians, pastors, educators, or business people. Everyone of us, by our conduct, our actions, our lifestyle, tries to play God. There is a measure of fatal conceit in all of us.

It is every man's trap, every woman's dilemma.

[1] Richard J. Foster, *Money, Sex, and Power* (New York, NY: Harper & Row, 1985).
[2] Ibid.
[3] A.W. Tozer, *The Pursuit of God* (Camp Hill, PA: Christian Publ., Inc., 1982).

4

The Arrogant Trap

> *The imbecility of men is always inviting the impudence of power.*
>
> Ralph Waldo Emerson

When things were going downhill for me and friends were few, I met Robert Lassiter. At the time, he was a popular radio talk-show host whose ratings for the "Drive Time" program in the metropolitan Tampa Bay area ranked at the top.

I accepted his invitation to be a guest on his show, and we had several hours of interesting and lively discussion about the world of televangelism. As a result, Mildred and I developed a friendship with Robert and his lovely wife, Mary.

As Robert's popularity continued to soar, he soon received an offer from the ABC Radio station, WLS, in America's third largest market, Chicago, Illinois. When the Lassiters left Tampa, our hearts were saddened, but we were excited for them and their new opportunity.

During my time of confinement in federal prison, we

kept in touch with our friends. After I was released and our lives returned to some normalcy, Mildred and I learned that Robert and Mary were no longer in Chicago. Robert's contract with the station had not been renewed, and they were living in Iowa.

After a short time, the Tampa market opened up for Robert again, and they moved back to the area. We made plans to visit with them and spent a wonderful evening renewing our friendship.

When I asked Robert what had happened in Chicago, he related to me the story of his exciting first evening in the Windy City. He and Mary had taken an apartment on the Gold Coast in Chicago — one of the most pricey addresses in The Loop.

On their first night there, the evening of August 15, 1989, he and Mary stood in their magnificent apartment on the fifteenth floor, gazing across that vast metropolis of over eight million people. Robert thought about his many successes and how he was now at the top of his profession.

As if surveying his domain, Robert looked out over Chicago and stated, "In two years, I will own this city!"

After he told me about that incident, Robert dropped his head and stared down at the floor. "Two years later, that city owned me!" he said somberly. "I was so arrogant. It never occurred to me that I might not be able to do it. Perhaps if I had developed a little more humility, it would have worked."

Robert's candor overwhelmed me. He honestly admitted what many of us have found to be true: It's our own arrogance that brings us down.

Setting the Trap

How does a person reach the place where he sees himself as invincible? Let me try to explain.

The adoration and acclaim showered on so-called "people of power" gives them the sense that they cannot fail.

The media surrounds them and clings to their every word. People seek their autographs, reach out to touch them, write fan mail, and praise their every action. In essence, they are treated as gods.

How would you react if people constantly picked up your check at the restaurant, opened every door, gave you the best seats, and sent you to the front of the line? Pretty soon you'd probably begin to expect such treatment and act out the part you're required to play.

High-profile leaders who are constantly in the public eye oftentimes act the way others expect them to act. This sense of importance eventually can make them feel bigger than God. With that kind of attitude, it doesn't take long before their values weaken, and they end up doing something illegal, immoral, or just plain stupid.

Because they are often surrounded by people who seek their approval, some begin to believe that most folks aren't too smart. After a while, they become isolated and can no longer relate to "the common man."

Convinced of their invincibility, they lose touch with themselves and take on an assumed personality. The real danger develops when they begin to believe they are better than everyone else.

As a result, they begin to make all the decisions because, they reason, "I am a winner. I know what is best. I don't need advice."

I know people involved in churches who look with disdain at others in their congregation. I have also seen businessmen badmouth customers, educators degrade students, flight attendants criticize their passengers, and church officials make light of their constituents' needs.

It's happened to all of us at one time or another. We begin to think we can cure every wrong, even when we have big problems ourselves. Manipulation takes hold, and we say to ourselves, *Others may be wrong, but I'm always right.*

The trap is now set, awaiting its unsuspecting prey.

Power and Public Opinion

Among the elites, public opinion plays almost no part. In fact, some treat public opinion as a monster that must be tamed so they can keep themselves in a power position. When a leader reaches that point, he is in a self-defeating state.

This arrogance of power is found in the home, in business, in education, in the media, in religion, and especially in politics.

Joseph Bailey, former president of David C. Cook Publishing Company, tells about an incident that occurred almost a year before Richard Nixon's resignation.

The president invited several advisors, including his son-in-law, to the Oval Office and asked what they thought he should do about Watergate.

David Eisenhower suggested that the American people are very forgiving. "Even at this date," he said, "if you went to them and said 'I did wrong, I'm sorry, please forgive me,' they would."

The president listened, then turned to the next person for his suggestion.

Joseph Bayly later said, "I'm inclined to agree with the advice David Eisenhower gave the president. I think that up until almost the very end, an admission of culpability and a plea for forgiveness would have been honored."

It's a tragedy President Nixon didn't listen to the counsel of his young son-in-law, who knew that contrition is always better than contention.

People in positions of power make mistakes. But sometimes our standards for judging leaders are too sweeping. We credit them for successes they didn't cause and blame them for problems they probably can't solve.

Some in positions of power, however, develop a concept of leadership that absolves them of responsibility. As a result, they constantly need to explain to the public their view of what leadership is supposed to be and why.

At the same time they are trying to win support, they maintain a contentious view of their constituents. Although trying desperately to manipulate popular opinion, their efforts appear transparently hypocritical and obviously unprincipled.

When the person in power realizes the error of his ways, he will try to change his image. But that often backfires because there is no base of trust among his subordinates or the public.

Who can forget the tear-stained face of Jimmy Swaggart sobbing from his pulpit? Our hearts broke to see the obvious pain and embarrassment over his exposed sin, but we couldn't help but question his motive and the sincerity of his confession.

When his sexual addiction surfaced again a few months later, our suspicions were heightened. Was his public display of repentance a ploy to win acceptance and approval? What were we to think when he refused to get the help he desperately needed? Was it pride and power, and not the prostitutes? Was that the problem?

It is any wonder the American people are so cynical about their leaders?

The Bottom Line

Unfortunately, those who initiate and aspire to power truly never enjoy the process of getting there. Why? Because they don't know for what purpose it was to be used. Their goals were all self-centered and self-serving.

Because they have no true vision and no desire to serve others, they become more concerned with stopping bad ideas than in promoting good ones. That's why some leaders confine their positions to subjects that lend themselves to quiet consensus — to areas that they already know will be approved. Such patrician, above-it-all, dictatorial leadership cripples creative thinking and quality effort.

People at the top of the heap often disdain change. New

ideas are feared and seen as a threat to their territory. It is not the new concepts they fear, however; it is the loss of power.

Roger Boisjoly worked as a senior engineer with Morton Thiokol, the company that manufactured the boosters and the rubber O-rings that seal the joint between the boosters and the fuel tanks on NASA space shuttles. An expert on rocket seals, Boisjoly had carefully monitored O-ring malfunctions at low temperatures and warned NASA and Thiokol against any launch when temperatures dropped below 35 degrees.

Chuck Colson and Jack Eckerd in their book, *Why America Doesn't Work,*[1] chronicled Boisjoly's account of one of the most devastating disasters in American history.

On January 27, 1986, the night before the Challenger launch, the Weather Bureau predicted a morning temperature of 18 degrees. Morton Thiokol's managers recommended the launch be scrubbed, but under pressure from NASA, the senior vice president decided to "take off his engineer's cap and put on his management cap."

Previously, Boisjoly had to prove that the flight was safe before the launch would be approved. Now management turned the tables. Boisjoly would have to prove that the seal would malfunction. In the end, management called Boisjoly's evidence "inconclusive," and approved the launch.

That night Boisjoly wrote in his journal, "I sincerely hope that this launch does not result in a catastrophe."

The next morning Boisjoly stood in the chilly air, watching the Challenger arc through the sky. At sixty seconds into its flight, he breathed a prayer of thanks. Thirteen seconds later, the enormous pressure of gases from the boosters blew past the rubber O-ring, still stiff with cold.

The Challenger exploded in mid-air.

Immediately, the question was asked: Who had approved the launch? The answer was clear: NASA was the client; NASA paid the bills; and NASA was tired of waiting.

What was the bottom line? Money, reputation, and

expediency were balanced against human life. As so often happens in a predatory society, the bottom line wins out.

That is the arrogance of power. There is no more accurate index to the failure of human nature than this abuse, misuse, and violation of trust and authority.

Prey for the Power Trap

As Pippert says, "Power is like money and sex — it's what you do with it that matters."[2]

Oliver North, a pivotal figure in the Iran-Contra affair during President Ronald Reagan's term in office, got caught in the power trap. While serving at the National Security Council in Washington, DC, he got an insider's view of American politics at its highest level.

"One of the most disenchanting aspects of the whole experience in Washington," he says, "was that so many people there are impressed with their own power. . . . There seems to be little purpose for many of them other than creating their own little fiefdoms."

Some people cannot see themselves in any other place than at the top of the heap. They are leaders, and that's the only way they will serve. They enjoy the prestige, the popularity, and the attention of being in the limelight. If they weren't leading the pack, they probably wouldn't have too much concern for service to God and to mankind.

That could never happen to me, you think. But don't fool yourself. As soon as you become arrogant in your ways — whether it's at home, in the office, or at church — the enemy considers you easy prey for his power trap.

Bruce W. Thielmann, pastor of First Presbyterian Church in Philadelphia, tells a story about his tenth-grade biology class.

One day his teacher made the class watch him feed a live white mouse to his pet four-foot boa constrictor he kept in a cage in the classroom.

When the students gathered around the cage, the shiny emerald-green serpent was lying casually in somewhat beautiful folds in one corner of the cage.

The teacher dropped a five-inch mouse into the cage. Totally unafraid, the mouse ran all around the cage, up over the snake, over the folds, and right in front of his face. It seemed to be having a grand old time. Then slowly but surely, the serpent began to move. It moved so slowly that the only way you could tell it was moving was to watch the lines of print on the newspapers at the bottom of the cage disappear beneath its head. The mouse noticed the movement, but it didn't seem to bother him.

Then, as the snake got closer, the mouse became fascinated. And as the snake moved stealthily, the mouse came to attention. Its tail wasn't stirring; it was totally engrossed in this moving green thing. It even sat up on its hind legs, holding its little paws in front of it like human hands. With its whiskers still twitching, the mouse sat there watching the snake come closer. Suddenly, there was a blur of green, and before anyone knew it, the snake had wrapped itself around the little mouse.

That's the way sin works, according to Thielmann. Its power lies in its ability to fascinate and mesmerize.[3]

The Motive of Power

If you didn't hold a position, how would you feel? Would you be lost without it? How far would you go to keep your position?

What are your motives? What are you committed to? Is it to God? Or to your work? Do you really care about people?

How much do you give of yourself in personally helping others? Or do you just like reigning at the top of the heap?

The question every leader should ask is, "Would I give the same commitment to this calling if I were not its leader? Would I be a Christian if I were not the head of this organization?"

Where would you be without a title? Whether it is president, manager, captain, foreman, pastor, deacon, teacher, or professor.

When some people lose their office, their job, or their title, they feel they've lost everything. Why? Because they are no longer in a position to exercise power over others.

Speaking recently before a businessmen's group, Oliver North said, "I considered myself the quintessential 'self-made man' on the fast track to a high-level position in the U.S. Marine Corps. It took a miracle to bring me face to face with a power greater than my own ambition. For all self-made men and women, God carries a two-by-four — and He uses it to get their attention."

That's a dangerous place to be.

As Oliver North and I can tell you: "It is a fearful thing to fall into the hands of the living God."

God loves us, and He will do everything possible — even if it means hitting us over the head — to keep us from tumbling through the trap door of arrogance and into the trap of self- destruction.

[1] Chuck Colson and Jack Eckerd, *Why America Doesn't Work*
[2] Wesley Pippert, *The Hand of the Mighty: Right and Wrong Uses of Our Power* (Grand Rapids, MI: Baker Book House/Revell, 1991).
[3] Robert L. Whitworth, *Windows* (Green Forest, AR: New Leaf Press, 1988), p. 37-38.

5

Fatal Conceit

*Power intoxicates men. It is never voluntar-
ily surrendered. It must be taken from them.*
                                    James F. Byrnes

During PTL's prime, the daily television broadcast had
a potential audience of about thirty million people. We were
wired into fifteen million homes, twenty-four hours a day,
and the PTL show was beamed out to 125 additional markets.

It's easy to get caught up in your own importance and
think you're top dog when you have an audience of millions
listening and clinging to your every word. Jim Bakker and
I weren't the only ones who let our egos get in the way of our
common sense, however.

One Sunday morning before the PTL scandal broke,
my wife and I were preparing for church and the television
was on in the bedroom.

Mildred, who had been listening, said to me, "Honey,
I think I just heard Brother Swaggart say something very
unusual."

Now my wife and I had known the Swaggarts for many

years and were close friends with them. In fact, on Jimmy and Frances' twenty-fifth wedding anniversary, we had been in Baton Rouge, Louisiana for the celebration and I had hosted the ceremonies for the huge banquet.

"What was it?" I asked, not surprised since Jimmy had been using his television program to lash out at PTL and Catholics and anyone who had doctrine contrary to his.

Mildred said that she thought she heard Jimmy Swaggart say that the Lord had told him that He would anoint *only* his ministry to win the world for Christ through television.

"Maybe you misunderstood," I said and then thought to myself, *No way would any preacher of the gospel ever make such a statement.*

As usual, Mildred didn't argue, but when my next copy of Jimmy Swaggart's magazine, *The Evangelist* arrived, there it was in black and white. Jimmy wrote that the Lord had told him God would anoint only his ministry to win the world for Christ through television.

The words leapt off the page and pierced my heart. I knew Jimmy believed it, and that's what worried me most. I also knew God would not let it go unnoticed.

At the time I had no idea that in a year or so I would be sitting in the Hilton Hotel in Baton Rouge at the request of our denominational superintendent in North Carolina. He had said, "You know, Richard, I think you and I should go down and meet with Jimmy Swaggart because he is so concerned about PTL. I've called and set up an appointment, but he wants you to be there, too."

At eleven o'clock in the morning, Jimmy, Frances, Donnie, and Jim Rentz entered the room for our meeting. For an hour and a half, Brother Swaggart ranted and raved against Jim Bakker and PTL. I didn't say a word.

Finally, he calmed down and said to me, "Maybe you've got something you want to say."

I had brought along a copy of the magazine article that said what Mildred had heard, and I handed it to him.

"No, Jimmy, you have something you need to say to us," I stated simply.

He looked at the article and then back at me and said, "Well, you guys aren't doing it."

"No, we're not," I replied. "Jimmy, God needs all of us. He divides His gifts severally as He wills."

I wasn't trying to be cute, but in my desperation I said, "Jimmy, this is not a McDonald's franchise. This is God's work. God needs all of us to do it."

God will have no part of our pride and arrogance. No matter how spiritual it appears. Shame on all of us if we take any delight in Jimmy Swaggart's failure. Shame on us also if we fail to learn from our own and other peoples failures. When Jimmy Swaggart submits to others, seeks help, asks to be forgiven by those he has hurt, and humbles himself, then freedom will come.

James Denney, a well-known English author said, "No man can give at once the impressions that he himself is clever and that Christ is mighty to save. If a person does not subdue this craving for attention and recognition, he will fall utterly short of the goal for which he was designed."

The Power Game

We live in a society that puts the premium on what we do rather than who we are. We judge ourselves by the kind of job we have, where we live, what we drive, and our status, rather than who we are.

No one asks, "What kind of parent are you ? Are you a decent person? How is your relationship to God?"

The first thing most people ask is, "What do you do?"

That was our big problem at PTL. We put the focus on what we were doing rather than on personal character.

It's so easy to point a finger at Richard Dortch, Jimmy Swaggart, Michael Milkin, and Ivan Boesky and say, "Isn't it terrible?"

And, you're right. We did do some things wrong. But

remember, you will never have to stand before God to answer for my sin or for the sins of anyone else. You will have to answer for your own sin.

Some think that because they're working in a religious organization or actively involved in their church or doing good deeds, that nothing like that could ever happen to them. Let me tell you something. When you get a haughty spirit, you are a prime target for the big fall.

Many of us, at some point in our lives, are caught up with the lust for power — "the fatal conceit." Columnist George Will wrote about it in *Newsweek* magazine.

This phrase, coined by Nobel prize winner, Friedrich von Hayek, denotes the tragedy that often accompanies power. The conceit results from the belief that by having power and becoming one of the governing elite, we can make the future conform to our plans.

With child-like reasoning, we consider the world to be putty in our hands and the future dependent only on our dreams. This conceit makes us believe we can treat people like Barbie dolls who serve only our whims and purposes. We play with their lives and their futures, making them act and think according to our desires.

In children, such reasoning is a beguiling attribute. Adults who seek to dominate others, however, often fail to come to grips with reality until it is too late. They do not understand what experience has taught many of us — that life sometimes deals very severely with our plans.

Psychologists say that as you get older, the more you will probably lust for power. It is our agenda that matters, and the results can be fatal.

It's all a part of the game of power.

Are You Power Hungry?

Who are the power hungry? How can we know if these tendencies are lying dormant in our own hearts just waiting for the right opportunity to surface?

Certain traits are common to most people who yearn for power. These characteristics are so well concealed behind a cloak of deception, however, that they are difficult to identify until after the lust for power has adversely affected its victim in some way.

Do any of these apply to you?

1. Your personal life contains hidden sins, either in conduct, decisions, or lifestyle.

The higher you get, the more territorial you become. To protect your position, your image, or your status, you begin hiding parts of your life. If you tell it the way it is, people will see your humanity, your flaws, and your authority may be called into question.

The way you deal with the sin in your life reveals the condition of your heart. Some people are only half awake. They feel moments of contrition because they are haunted by impure dreams, and yet are perfectly unconscious that their lives are one long expression of envy, malice, hatred, and uncharitableness. Others are sexually impure, and yet haunted with remorse for an unkind word.

An illustration from a book called *Windows* reveals the danger of small sins.

> A cow in Greenwood, Maine, met with a remarkable accident. She jumped over a fence, stumbled on the other side, and fell on her head. Her horns ran under the root of a tree, and thus her head was held down. Her nose was submerged in a little pool of water, only an inch or two deep, but she was held to it, and it was dangerous as an ocean of water would have been. She was found dead . . . drowned in a puddle.
>
> I have read of a similar accident that happened to an elderly lady. She was very feeble, and while tottering outside one day, she fell with her

mouth and nose in a tiny puddle. She was too weak to turn over and thus she also died.

Now anyone may see that this drowning in a puddle is a very common occurrence. Although, of course I do not mean the literal happening, but rather its spiritual counterpart. For it does not need a big sin to drown a soul; we often think it does. We often think that, as long as our sins do not run in black waves, mountain high, or stretch out in a devastating flood, or descend in the irresistible plunge of Niagara, we are perfectly safe.[1]

2. You fail to speak up when you know something is wrong because you want to protect your own position.

You are always reluctant to take a stand in case the outcome does not work to your advantage.

Do you have a numbed conscience about some things that are right and wrong? You are always so sure you are right that it never occurs to you that your silence is wrong.

The *Westminster Larger Catechism* bears witness to our treacherous hearts:

> We regard the wicked according to the work of the righteous, and the righteous according to the work of the wicked; forgery, concealing the truth, undue silence in a just cause, and holding our peace when inequity calleth for either a reproof from ourselves, or complaint to others; speaking the truth unseasonably, or maliciously to a wrong end, or perverting it to a wrong meaning, or in doubtful and equivocal expressions to the prejudice of truth or justice . . . raising false rumors, receiving and countenancing evil reports, and stopping our ears against just defense . . . .

We are commanded not to leave things undone that we know are right. We must take seriously the harm that others bring to the flock of humanity. We cautiously must alert people and humbly hope that we are reminded of our own words when we see the errors of others.

We need this instruction because someday we shall stand before the blazing glory of God on judgment day honestly, and we will bring forth ourselves, and every knee shall bow.

3. You take advantage of the failures of others.

The lowest and most deceptive use of power takes advantage of a weaker person.

In my hurting and grieving moments after PTL, I wanted desperately to be accepted. One day I inquired of a friend, who was a denominational official, about another church officer. "Do you think he could accept me with all that has been written and said about me?" I asked, hoping to find love and forgiveness at a time when I desperately needed it.

My friend replied honestly, "He might, but only if it makes him look good. He will help you, if it helps him; otherwise, forget it."

I felt as if a snake had crawled out from under a rock and sunk his fangs into my flesh. The pain that gripped my heart was no less. I grieved, not only for the rejection I had just experienced but for my brother's pride and selfishness that — I knew — God would not let go unattended.

4. You have conflicts of interest.

Christians in positions of leadership should avoid conflicts of interest at all cost, especially in areas where finances and personal interest are intertwined.

Legislators and judges are mandated by law to separate their personal business from their official duties. Certainly those of us who are trying to live a life above reproach will strive to be above board, unless, of course, we are seeking power.

We have lived in the Tampa Bay area long enough to pick up on the incidents of the rough and tumble politics of the Sun Coast of Florida. When the St. Petersburg, Florida, city commission recently voted on a multi-million dollar bond issue, Mayor David Fischer decided he could not vote on the proposal. The reason? His daughter was employed by the company helping the city sell the issue. Even though she worked for the same company in a distant city and the bond offering was relatively small, the mayor would not do it. He wanted to avoid any appearance of conflict of interest.

Such, however, is not always the case.

Recently, members of the board of directors of a church organization voted on a financial issue that affected almost everyone on the board. They denied the claims of several people, and their vote kept money in their own account that would have paid the claims. They were clearly voting on an issue that affected their own funds.

When those responsible were confronted they would not show the Christian courtesy of a response. They were above it all. They would not address their own conduct, their own conceit.

Reinhold Niebuhr says, "We have two motives: the one we publish, and the real one. Good people want to do the selfish thing, but they don't until they find an unselfish reason for doing it."

5. You deceive yourself and others.

Illicit power is gained through deceptive means because you must convince yourself and others that you are number one.

To be a person of sought-after power you have to lie a lot. After a while it gets easy. Once you've learned to lie to yourself, lying to others becomes the natural thing to do.

Deceptive power has as a part of its foundation the

breaking of the ninth commandment. It is the ultimate "false witness against thy neighbor."

You prejudice the truth and the good name of your neighbors, as well as your own. You give false evidence and produce false witnesses. You promote evil causes, always crying that you speak the truth. You pass out unjust sentences and call evil works good; and good, evil.

6. You have a haughty spirit.

Arrogance, power, and lying walk hand in hand. They belong to the same gang, and they protect their turf by deception.

You are responsible to no one. Your motto is: If it feels good, do it! As long as you get what you want, that's all that matters.

You have fooled yourself and others to believe that you are equal with God. You would never say so, of course, but you demonstrate it in your daily walk. Your arrogance shows in the way you do business and as you go about grabbing for power. Because of the void within, you assume that what you want is what is best for yourself and others.

7. You will lie or do whatever is necessary to retain your place of power.

I know from personal experience and from the observation of others that power that is sought will pay any price.

When you hunger after power — when it is what you think about a lot — then you begin to manipulate situations and people in your own mind. You make comparisons continually and strive to always come out on top. You must be number one. When you crave power, you will lie to get it, to keep it, and to get more.

The lust for power is like lava cascading from a fiery volcano. It will destroy anyone and everything that gets in its way.

Surrender

Why do you seek power? Because you have not surrendered yourself.

The last thing any of us want to let go of is ourselves. We think it is the one and only thing that we can own.

Jesus said, "If any man come to me and hate not his father, and mother, and wife, and children, and brethren, and sisters, yea, and his own life also, he cannot be my disciple" (Luke 14:26).

Everything must come before Him and be given to God. This does not mean that we should leave our family. When our Lord used the word "hate" the meaning is to "love less."

A lighted candle, when it is put before a high powered electric light, casts a shadow. Lesser loves, while really light, cast a shadow when this all-consuming love makes its demand upon us.

In the Scripture above, the last thing that Jesus mentioned was, "his own life, also." Why does He put our life last? Because it is the last thing we ever give up.

"Millions for an inch of time!" cried Elizabeth, the gifted but ambitious queen of England, upon her deathbed. The unhappy woman was reclining upon a royal couch with ten thousand dresses in her wardrobe and a kingdom on which the "sun never sets" at her feet. All were now valueless, and she shrieked in vain for a single "inch of time!"

She had enjoyed threescore and ten years. Like too many of us, she had so devoted her life to wealth, pleasure, pride, and ambition, that her whole preparation for eternity was crowded into her final moments; hence she, who had wasted more than half a century, would barter millions for an inch of time.[2]

Maybe you realize that you are overly concerned about position, place, and power. Maybe you've sacrificed a great deal to get to where you are today. But is your place and position what God desires for you? Or is there so much vanity and personal ambition mixed up in your motives that you're not sure? Is self still strutting around the altar of sacrifice? If so, it must be surrendered.

It is at this point and place that the real battle occurs. Everything else is just a skirmish.

We are never more right with God than when we are examining ourselves.

When you seek power, you are really expressing your deepest fears about yourself. Deep within, you are actually very much afraid. Search your heart and mind. Do you have vague inward fears about poverty, sickness, failure, and death?

You can be free, but it will cost you something.

[1]Robert L. Whitworth, *Windows* (Green Forest, AR: New Leaf Press, 1988), p. 58.
[2]Ibid., p. 21.

6

Deadly Jealousy

*From the summit of power men no longer
turn their eyes upward, but begin to look about
them.*

James Russell Lowell

In 1977, Robert J. Ringer hit the best-seller list with his book, *Looking Out for Number One.*[1] This people's philosopher of the seventies guided his readers on "the most exciting and rewarding journey of their lives" with such thoughts as this: "Man's primary moral duty lies in the pursuit of pleasure, so long as he does not forcibly interfere with the rights of others."

According to Ringer, people act in their own self interests all of the time anyway, so the best, most honorable solution comes when we confront that desire and use it. Ringer's philosophy of self interest is certainly not unique. Selfishness and hedonistic activities, laced with mega doses of greed and jealousy, and clothed in positive, success oriented phrases, have become "healthy" and fashionable trends in recent years.

Is it any wonder that the most popular books have envy-producing, narcissistic slogans like:

"Looking out for number one."

"Winning through intimidation."

"Power isn't everything, it is the only thing."

"You can have it all."

"If you have money and power, you can make all your dreams come true."

Popular songs also reflect this "fashionable" trend. Country singer, Tom T. Hall, in singing about his philosophy of life, condenses it down to six profound words: Faster horses, younger women, more money.

Entertainers and authors are not alone in their power hungry doctrines. Today's governments are also ripe with jealousy and greed. Millions continue to die in wars waged because of controversy sparked by this malice. Compulsive extravagance and related jealousies have reached epidemic stages.

According to Richard J. Foster, "The contemporary lust for more, more, more is clearly psychotic. It has completely lost touch with reality. The chasm between Third World poverty and First World affluence is accelerating at an alarming rate."[2]

Foster also pointed to the rampant lust for "more" in all segments of society. The idolatry of today is the idolatry of power. Books by the score appeal to our Machiavellian passions.

There are some political leaders who give more energy to jockeying for position than to serving the public good, and some business executives care more for staying on top of the heap than for producing a useful product. Some university professors seek sophistication more than truth, and there are those religious leaders care more for their image than for the gospel.

Where It All Started

Let's face it — the idea of being *numero uno,* of having power, success, money, and prestige is very beguiling and attractive.

That idea has been at the heart of evil since Lucifer looked around at what he had and compared it to what belonged to God. He felt short-changed by the hand he'd been dealt.

Has anything really changed from the moment Eve looked upon the fruit and believed the serpent's line which, in effect, was this: "You've got to look out for number one, girl. God is holding out on you. You've got to reach for your own brass ring. You really can have it all."

Jealousy also clouded Cain's mind from the truth. As a result, his brother Abel's blood ran onto the cursed soil, and history was altered tragically.

The themes of jealousy, envy, and covetousness have run like a green rage throughout the centuries.

Joseph's brothers were envious of their father Jacob's favor, and covetous of the favorite son role. Right or wrong, Jacob chose Joseph for a special place in the family. God, by foreknowledge, gave the dreams to Joseph who unknowingly was being prepared for coming sufferings and triumphs.

Jealousy is often based upon fear — fear of losing something. Jealousy is always a selfish emotion.

Joseph's brothers lost face when God gave their younger sibling dreams. Then when Jacob presented Joseph with the multi-colored coat, the brothers' pride and self-love were wounded, thereby producing a need for retaliation. Joseph, as he walked to Shechem, was an easy target for their collective streams of jealous hatred.

Jealousy has as inherent ingredients all three things that make up the world system of evil and rebellion against God: ". . . the lust of the flesh, and the lust of the eyes, and the pride of life" (1 John 2:16).

The lust of the flesh produces covetousness, witch-craft, idolatry, hatred, and jealous emulations.

The lust of the eyes finds expression in sexual lust, covetousness, idol worship, and evil practices.

The pride of life displays its arrogance in self-righteousness and a desire for position, power, riches, and strength, glorying in hedonistic activities.

Do we, as twentieth century Christians, have a right to waggle our fingers at Lucifer or even Joseph's brothers? Let's face it; we all have a secret flame burning to "have it all." And if we cannot have all we want, we are satisfied to merely dethrone those who seem to epitomize health, wealth, and success.

The Spirit of Jealousy

At the root of this age-old lust for money, sex, and power is that emerald menace.

According to the Book of Numbers, there is an actual "spirit of jealousy." It seems to have overtaken us Christians perhaps to a greater extent than many of the "sinners" recorded in the Bible. In retrospect, the sin of the brothers against Joseph seems rather tame compared to today's narcissistic society.

Dostoyevsky, in his masterpiece *The Idiot*,[3] thrust a Christ-like figure, Prince Myshkin, into a culture obsessed with wealth, power, and sexual conquest. But Myshkin's selfless and angelic behavior was so abnormal that the people, though touched by his innocence and simplicity, finally concluded that he was, as the title implies, naive and intelligently deficit.

Jealousy breeds a menacing harvest of greed, rebellion, injustice, and death. When the "have nots" rage with envy against the people perceived to be "haves", war explodes. Alexander the Great, Napoleon, Hitler, and Ho Chi Minh built vast war machines fueled by jealousy.

The atrocities committed against the Native Americans and African-Americans reflect this same lustful disease.

Jealousy runs rampant today in Afghanistan, Nicaragua, and Cambodia. It greatly affects Europe, and has deeply imbedded itself in the United States.

Likewise, jealousy seethes among Christian ranks. Splits and divisions erupt because of covetousness. Ministries rail against the growth of other ministries. Nothing would make some segments of the church happier than for one of the large media ministries to go bankrupt. (Inwardly, of course, a pious, caring front is always displayed.)

Where will it end?

It Will Rot Your Bones

God warned us against jealousy and envy.

"Envy thou not the oppressor, and choose none of his ways" (Prov. 3:31).

"A sound heart is the life of the flesh; but envy the rottenness of the bones" (Prov. 14:30).

"Let us not be desirous of vain glory, provoking one another, envying one another" (Gal. 5:26).

God did not warn us lightly. He knew the results of unbridled jealousy, envy, and covetousness.

Dr. S.I. McMillan, a medical doctor, revealed startling facts in his revolutionary book, *None of These Diseases*. He writes:

Centuries before modern psychiatry discovered that carnal emotions were important factors in the causation of many psychosomatic diseases, the Bible condemned these emotions and provided a cure for them. "The activities of the lower nature are quarreling, jealousy, bad temper, rivalry, factions, party spirit, envy, drunkenness, orgies, and things like that" (Gal. 5:19-21). "Those who belong to Christ have crucified the flesh with its emotions and passions" (Gal. 5:24).[4]

Dr. McMillan goes on to list over fifty diseases caused by emotional stress. Many of which related directly to jealousy.
Tim LaHaye says:

> That answers for me the question that has been asked many times by rebellious, bitter Christians: "Why has God permitted all this sickness to come into my life?" It seems from these medical findings that in most cases God didn't "permit" it. Personal anger (sin) caused it.

Even Shakespeare knew enough of the Bible and psychiatry to recognize that people can become sick from unconfessed sin, especially jealousy. It was envy and covetousness that caused the murder of Duncan, and the memory of that jealous act produced psychosomatic overtones in Lady Macbeth. When her husband asked the physician about her illness the doctor replied, "Not so sick, my lord, as she is troubled with thick coming fancies that keep her from her rest."

Waiting to understand more, Macbeth then asked the same question still put to many a physician and minister today: "Canst thou not minister to mind disease, pluck from the memory a rooted sorrow, raise out written troubles of the brain, and with some sweet oblivious antidote cleanse the stuffed bosom of that perilous stuff which weighs upon the heart?"

Shakespeare, however, has no answer. But God does.

The Antidote

There are several anti-toxins to jealousy, namely forgiveness, right thinking, contentment, positive action, and giving. But they are incomplete ingredients in the one great antidote: agape love. Spontaneous and divine, it is more eternal than the most deadly poisons.

Love is more than the opposite of jealousy — it is God's cure, as passionately related in 1 Corinthians 13. Allow me to paraphrase it for you:

Love is patient. It is unhurried, long suffering, bearing, believing, hoping, and enduring all things.

Love is kind. Kindness is love in action, never rash, insolent, inconsistent, puffed up, or proud.

Love is generous. It loves even during competition without envy or jealousy.

Love is humble. It does not preen nor parade even when it could be smugly self-righteous.

Love is courteous, it is social, always polite, at home with all social strata, never rude nor discourteous.

Love is unselfish, never bitter. It seeks only the good of others and it does not retaliate or seek revenge even when humanly justified.

Love is good tempered. It does not get irritated and is never resentful even through injustice.

Love is righteous. It conducts itself without hate or sin. It is never glad when others go wrong, always gladdened by goodness to others, always slow to expose, always eager to believe the best, always hopeful, and always enduring.

Love is sincere. It is never boastful or conceited. It is always honest, leaving no impression but that which is strictly true, never blazes out in passionate anger, never broods over wrong, is always just, joyful, and truthful, and knows how to be trusted and silent.

What a contrast. Love is the one and only antidote that can save mankind from jealousy.

Psychiatrist Smiley Blanton emphasized this fact in his book, *Love or Perish:* Without love, unjealous consideration of others, man would likely perish from a variety of mental and physical diseases."[5]

Alfred Adler, the internationally known psychiatrist, after careful analysis of thousands of patients wrote,

> The most important task imposed by religion has always been "Love thy neighbor." It is the individual who is not interested in his fellow man who has the greatest difficulty in life and provides the greatest injury to others. It is from among such individuals that all human failures spring.[6]

Jesus Christ came to give us not only eternal life when we die, but abundant life here and now. That life can only be experienced by abiding in Him. No man can abide in Christ or be filled with the Spirit who grieves the Holy Spirit. Anger, bitterness, wrath, clamor, and the enmity of heart grieve the Holy Spirit of God.

Life is a constant, countless series of choices. Jealousy and its resultant nemesis sprout from wrong decisions, and once rooted become nearly impossible to remove. Once grown they yield one disastrous harvest after another.

Joseph and his brothers became graphic examples. Compare the brothers' tragedies to Joseph's unjealous life.

Love is the only antidote to jealousy. If we are to survive as a people, then our society must make a judgment of jealousy, and it must begin in the house of the Lord. Jealousy's seed is planted deeply there.

> For you, brethren, were [indeed] called to freedom; only [do not let your] freedom be an incentive to your flesh and an opportunity or

excuse [for selfishness], but through love you should serve one another. For the whole Law [concerning human relationships] is complied within the one precept, you shall love your neighbor as [you do] yourself. But if you bite and devour one another [in partisan strife] be careful that you [and your whole fellowship] are not consumed by one another (Gal. 5:13-15;AMP).

Many of our problems are a direct result of a jealous heart. We must firmly look at ourselves. Let me ask you:

How do you respond when someone is preferred before you?

When someone fails, do you feel vindicated — that you are living proof that you were really better and that is why you have not failed?

When someone you regard as inferior to you seems to be blessed beyond your expectation, can you rejoice with them?

What about jealousy — has it gotten into you?

Jealousy is a vicious, mind-altering emotion. It is so deep within us that we may need help to find true deliverance from its pangs.

[1]Robert J. Ringer, *Looking Out for Number One* (New York, NY: Fawcett Juniper, 1985).
[2]Richard J. Foster, *Money, Sex, and Power* (New York, NY: Harper & Row, 1985).
[3]Fyodor Dostoyevsky, *The Idiot* (New York, NY: Penguin USA, 1956).
[4]S.I. McMillan, *None of These Diseases* (Grand Rapids, MI: Baker Book House/Revell, 1985).
[5]Smiley Blanton, *Love or Perish*
[6]Alfred Adler

7

Beyond Accountability

Power must never be trusted without a check.
John Adams

As the PTL scandal unfolded and our world began to unravel, spectators both in Christian and secular society began gathering under the banner of accountability. "If there had only been greater accountability," was their mantra, chanted in churches and on network news alike.

For almost three years I sat on the sidelines and watched the charade of institutions, ministries, and individuals scream, "We're okay. Just look at our books." Some couldn't wait until they could relate how honest they were.

Was it concern for accountability or an attempt to cover their rear flank?

We seldom use the word "accountability" properly any longer. Today accountability generally refers to bookkeeping — being able to show a clean set of financial records. We even have our religious versions of the Good Housekeeping Seal of Approval to put on our organization's letterhead and publications to prove to our contributors we are worthy of their money.

Take it from someone who has been at the top of such an organization, these emblems and symbols can be merely veneer covering a structure that is rotten with neglect and abuse.

After the publication of my book, *Integrity, How I Lost It and My Journey Back*[1], I received a number of calls from prominent people, some who worked in businesses, secular organizations, and in ministries saying, "I didn't think you knew that much about our procedures. But apparently you did."

I had to assure them I knew nothing about their corporate operation.

"But the book read like you were describing our organization," one man told me. "I, too, have compromised my integrity. You have defined exactly how our place operates on a smaller scale."

I wondered how that could be when I knew their organization had a very high "accountability rating" and had acquired the evangelical seal of approval.

While preaching one night in a large city I experienced one of those "made to know" moments. I stopped speaking and listened to my heart. I shocked myself by saying, "I believe there is someone here who has sold their integrity for power and money. You have lied to keep your job. You had better stop it now."

At the end of the service, the pastor motioned toward a man near the door saying, "He's waiting to talk to you."

After I greeted the man, he told me, "I'm the one you were talking about tonight. For years I have been the chief financial officer of a nationally known religious organization. I have lied to keep my job. I have to do it."

"You should resign tomorrow morning, my friend,"

was my counsel.

Born Again Accountability

It is socially acceptable to have the appearance of accountability among our peers, but what we really ought to be concerned about is honesty within.

For most people "accountability" has lost its meaning in the same way "born again" has become a generic term for the world to use. Driving through almost any city these days you can see Born-Again Bookstores, Born-Again Used Cars, and Born-Again Hairstylists. Of course this is far from the original intent of the phrase to be "born again" of the Holy Spirit.

The same thing has happened to the idea of accountability. Properly used, accountability means: *being obligated for your actions and responsible for what you do.*

Many attempts at accountability, both by individuals and corporations, really mean, "Accept me as I present myself to be. Don't ask any questions. Don't look beyond what I show you."

Does the structure of accountability make people accountable?

The issue today is not to simply present some kind of a front. Instead, we must go beyond accountability. We must no longer be satisfied with just having financial records that will pass cursory inspection. Instead, we must demand of ourselves — personally and corporately — responsibility in all our words and actions.

One television preacher who heads a university was recently assessed $120,000, then $50,000 by the IRS for using his political operation as a part of his tax exempt work. In addition, the accrediting association for his university cited him for offering more off-campus collegiate work than he was authorized to do. To make matters worse, a television station in Tampa, Florida, is bringing suit against this pastor's church for tens of thousands of dollars of air time he has refused to pay since 1990.

This preacher's foolish actions have undermined his ministry with the government, the community, and the public. It is not the message he preaches that is the problem; it is the power he seeks and the lack of true accountability.

Executive Privilege

Recently, the entire House of Representatives was called upon to account for its abuse of power concerning congressional perks — most noticeably the house bank and the house post office. Some congressmen stood up and confessed to overstepping the bounds of their authority.

The majority of our representatives, however, simply said, "People in our position have been doing this for a long time, and we deserve the same privileges." Accountability no longer has any meaning in a situation like this.

The biggest obstacle in the path beyond accountability is power.

At the slightest taste of power, our senses are often dulled to our responsibility. A position of power seems to tell us we are above accountability — that we owe no one an explanation for what we say or do. Just being in a position of authority somehow gives us the sense that we are above the rules. When called on to give account for our actions, we claim executive privilege.

Richard Nixon claimed executive privilege to prevent having to answer for his role in political espionage and the subsequent cover-up of Watergate.

Generally we don't want anyone to know the whole story because our accountability factor doesn't run too deep. There are too many theatrics involved in the whole process today. Because of this, people are pretty well resolved that they are being taken.

Organizations say, "Here are my books. You can see that one and one adds up to two, but don't ask me how I got the one and one — I may not want you to know."

A number of years ago church growth expert Elmer Towns wrote a book describing the growth and development of the ten largest Sunday schools in the United States.

One of the pastors whose church was among the top ten said, in a public meeting, that seven of the ten pastors from those churches did not report their figures accurately.

How does that make you feel?

If we can't trust pastors to report accurately the number of children attending their Sunday schools, whom can we trust? Is anybody telling the truth?

Former *New York Times* columnist Hedrick Smith said, "In the intangible chemistry of power no quality matters more than trust."

The bulk of us, in and out of the church, government, industry, education, and in our relationships in society are in denial. We don't really want to know the truth. We want to be placated with things that fit our preconceived ideas and our current modes.

Elmer Towns, himself a Baptist, once suggested, "Our reports indicate there are more Baptists than people."

If all the missions reports submitted to church boards were to be believed, the world would have been saved several times over by now.

Power brings the impression that the end justifies the means. We must go beyond accountability to truth.

Behind Closed Doors

Too much of our work is done behind closed doors. "There is only one question of paramount importance in the Christian light," Dietrich Bonhoeffer declared, "and that is, how shall we survive the last judgment?" [2]

It's easy for people to talk about accountability, providing they do not have to be accountable. One of the questions I have to ask is: "When I am accountable to those over me, to whom are my superiors accountable? Where is their accountability? To whom are they submitting, as I am, in a daily relationship?"

Yet, where is their accountability? I will admit my sins, my errors, and my misjudgment, but will they?

Not only do they fail to face their own weaknesses, people of power generally fail to discipline their peers — the ones they work with from day to day. Yet, they will confront others across the country or across the state, but how about those across the table? That is where it counts.

It's true in business.

It's true in government.

It's true in education.

It's true in the church.

When it's one of our own, it's tough to go against the tide. But, at least, let's recognize that there is a problem in this area.

When things are being said that are not right, no one wants to rock the boat. But when we go along, are we giving in and giving up a part of our own integrity? When we get together as a group, do we ever have the courage to speak up and say, "What we are doing is not right!"

I have had leaders tell me they knew certain issues being discussed within their group were not right. Later I would learn that, when their group met, these same leaders voted unanimously to do the very things they had previously told me were wrong.

A Lying Tongue

James Patterson and Peter Kim make some startling revelations in their book, *The Day America Told the Truth.*[3] The facts, taken from the largest survey ever done on the subject of the morals of the American public, tell us: men lie more than women; young men lie more than older men; and unemployed people lie more than those with jobs.

One person explained, "Lying is a way of gaining power over other people through manipulating them in various ways. It's something that everybody does."

Who are Americans lying to? Here's the breakdown:

86 percent lie to parents,
75 percent to friends,
73 percent to siblings,
69 percent to spouses,
58 percent to best friends,
49 percent to neighbors,
32 percent to doctors,
21 percent to clergymen, and
20 percent to lawyers.

The research states firmly that there are more serious liars today than at any time in our nation's past:

> Lying has become a cultural trait in America. Lying is imbedded in our national character. That really hasn't been understood around the world. Americans lie about everything — and usually for no good reason.
>
> The majority of Americans today (two in every three) believe that there is nothing wrong with telling a lie. Only 31 percent of us believe that honesty is the best policy.

Lying is a habit. Little lies and white lies develop into big lies and all different colors of lies. Businessmen, entertainers, ministers, carpenters, college professors, students, housewives — all do it. Some do it very well. Even institutions do it. We do it to impress people. Most of us find it difficult sometimes not to embellish the facts and to simply tell the truth.

God hates a lying tongue; despises lying indiscriminately; detests barefaced, bold lying — yet 91 percent of the American people do it on a regular basis.

David pleaded to be free from lying lips: "Deliver my

soul, O Lord, from lying lips, and from a deceitful tongue" (Ps. 120:2).

After I wrote the book *Integrity, How I Lost It and My Journey Back,* I received hundreds of letters from people from all over the world. Many expressed that I had pointedly addressed the lack of integrity in their own private lives, their churches, their ministries, their businesses, and their professional lives.

One of the most interesting and fascinating letters came from a missionary. I'm sure his experience is not unusual.

During his earlier days on the mission field, this young man had wanted to make sure every project he undertook was completed with honesty and integrity and purity of heart. It didn't take long, however, for his values to shift. As the pressure from his peers to construct more churches and buildings increased, financing the many projects became his main focus.

Another missionary told him about an easy way to raise funds. "Just tell the folks back home you need money to put a roof on a church."

In his letter to me, he wrote, "In my quest for power, I laid aside my honesty, and on one occasion raised the money for one church roof 24 times!"

Now in an effort to come to grips with himself and what he had done, he realized it was far better to raise the money for one roof, and do it in an honest fashion, than to attempt to meet quotas set by others.

When Greed Takes Over

Misplaced power often results from greed. All too often well-intentioned people in positions of power say to themselves, "I have worked hard for a long time. I deserve something more than I am currently getting as a reward." As a result, greed takes over.

The prisons are full of otherwise decent people who got

greedy. I know because I became friends with many of them. Some had been lawyers, businessmen, doctors — even former FBI agents. One man had been a United States federal judge and another a member of President Reagan's secret service detail.

One inmate explained to me how he let greed ruin his life.

"I had $650,000 in the bank and a prosperous business," he said. "Then one of the guys who worked for me asked if he could use my vehicle for one week. He said he'd give me $25,000. I didn't need the money. I could have sold the business and probably made another half million, but I had to have more."

He was sentenced to six and a half years for his part in a drug deal. Believe me, it can happen to anybody whose heart is controlled by greed.

Each week when the federal bureau prison's bus pulled up in front of the prison, I watched as the khaki-clad group of prisoners descended with feet shackled, hands in cuffs, and chains linking them together. Repeatedly, I asked myself the question, "Has the lust for power so permeated our society that each week bus loads of otherwise normal citizens are taken to prisons all across America?"

How did they get to this point in their lives? It was the feeling, the quest, the belief that they were above it all and could do as they pleased and never be held accountable for their conduct or actions. It was the power they sought at any cost.

Honest Questions

Is it possible to be a power seeker and still be truthful?

E. Stanley Jones, the master teacher, raises questions about power and truth, in his book *The Christ of Every Road*.[4]

Ask yourself these questions:

1. Do I tell the truth under all circumstances? Will I always be truthful regardless of the consequences?

2. Am I honest in all facets of my life? Will I cheat if it is a better deal? Would I hurt someone to advance myself?

3. Am I really a pure person? In every circumstance, is my mind under control? Would I do things in private that could bring shame to my life?

4. Do I have a loving spirit? Am I a loving person in my attitude and my temper? Am I easily offended?

5. Am I making selfish decisions? Do I really live for myself, or others? Do I take advantage of people by my decisions?

These are sobering, self-revealing questions that tell us much about ourselves. Are we being taken in by a fatal conceit?

The Psalmist asks, "Lord, who shall abide in thy tabernacle? who shall dwell in thy holy hill? He that walketh uprightly, and worketh righteousness, and speaketh the truth in his heart" (Ps. 15:1-2).

If we want God's presence in our lives, lying has to go! The power game must be finished! We must repent of our sin of deceitfulness.

Jesus revealed the source of all lies when he told the Pharisees, "Ye are of your father, the devil . . . for he is a liar, and the father of it" (John 8:44). As with all sin, when we lie, we align ourselves with the devil.

God wants to take us beyond accountability to total honesty — with Him, with others, and with ourselves.

[1]Richard Dortch, *Integrity, How I Lost It and My Journey Back* (Green Forest, AR: New Leaf Press, 1992).

[2]Dietrich Bonhoeffer, *Life Together* (San Francisco, CA: Harper San Francisco, 1992).

[3]James Patterson and Peter Kim, *The Day America Told the Truth* (New York, NY: Prentice Hall Press, 1991).

[4]E. Stanley Jones, *The Christ of Every Road* (Nashville, TN: Abingdon Press, 1930).

8

Power in the Church

*There is a strain in a man's heart that will
sometime or other run out to excess, unless the
Lord restrain it, but it is not good to venture it: it
is necessary therefore, that all power that is on
earth be limited, church-power or other.*

John Cotton

One day as I drove to a remote town in the Midwest, I
wearily considered my next assignment.

That evening I was to meet with the leaders of a church
that for years had experienced internal conflict. I had been
forewarned by the pastor that a certain member of their
governing body would not carry out the wishes of the rest of
the group.

It was hard for me to believe that a Christian brother
could be so dictatorial that he would refuse to listen to
anyone in his church — including the pastor. That's why I
had been called in to assess the situation. As the highest
elective denominational officer in the state at that time, it
was up to me to challenge him.

As the meeting began, the pastor explained, "Pastor Dortch is here as a guest to participate with us in our monthly meeting."

I listened attentively as the church financial statement and other issues were discussed as part of normal business.

Then one of the members of the board made a motion to grant a certain sum of money for a particular need. When the vote was taken, out of the corner of my eye, I saw one of the members begin to speak. I thought I heard him say, "I won't write the check."

I did not respond, but after a few moments of silence, I spoke up and said, "I think I heard someone say, following the passage of this recent motion, that he wouldn't write the check."

A large, well-built man pulled himself up and replied, "Yes, I said it. I won't write the check to give that money they just voted on."

After I caught my breath, I regained my composure and simply stated, "Well, sir, if that's the case, then we would be willing to accept your resignation. Your unwillingness to follow what the board has decided makes you unqualified for the office."

For a moment, the man appeared stunned, but then he stomped out of the room.

I could see that this man had some very deep-seated problems, but I knew he had to be removed from office for the sake of the church.

"How did things get to this point?" I asked the minister.

"This man had been bullying everybody on the board long before I became the pastor," he explained. "As you can see, all he needed was to be challenged."

It happens all the time — in every business, organization, government agency, educational institution, church, and oftentimes at the workplace. Someone will lift himself up and by his physical presence, his loud voice, or his willingness to speak up, do something completely unconventional and out of order. The rest of us stand back and wonder how a person could have such gall.

We have a name for people like that — bullies. They demand to be heard and are convinced that any group of people, committee, board, or God, cannot accomplish any-thing unless *they* speak to the issue. They are arrogant, inflated, self-deceived people.

Bullies

Many businessmen, politicians, professionals, educa-tors, and yes, even people like me, want to be known as Christians. But, let's face it,some folks are not nice people. They are bullies who take advantage of others, threatening and dominating people in their madness for power.

Bullies do not consider what's best for all concerned, instead they seek a position of power from which they can dominate others. They are pompous at the work place and take advantage of their position of power to maintain con-trol. You see them in service agencies, government offices, classrooms, businesses, ministries, churches, and in the pulpits.

I know bullies in business, government, education, and ministry who do not treat people with dignity and who look with disdain on anyone who does not agree with them. They do not listen to the views of others and care only about getting credit for things that make them look good.

In a financial crisis, some will take advantage of people to bully them into giving. In so doing, they think they are serving the Lord because their cause is just.

People sometimes use others to advance and exalt their own agenda. When we become power seekers, power bro-kers, and attention-getters, all that matters is our program and our ministry. Political office seekers often use the same tactics.

Sometimes the situation is reversed, and a congrega-tion will gang up on their pastor. Or citizens will become intoxicated with power and complain to business or government about issues they want resolved for their own personal benefit. What they really seek is power.

Others, serving on church boards or in places of leadership, will abuse their power by using it against other people in a congregation. When people have hidden agendas, and when non-disclosure is standard operating procedure, the perfect environment is created for bullies to push people around.

We've all met people with that kind of attitude: Either you do it my way, or I will make your life miserable.

Such people think God cannot do anything unless He checks with them first — and still, they must have the last word. Some of them fake it and cry, "God has given me some special gift," or "I am a prophet." They say they want to be involved in spiritual warfare when in fact, at the core, they are bullies trying to lord it over people. They are false prophets who are in a mindset of grandeur, and they need to be brought to reality.

The only way to deal with bullies is to get things out in the open. They are always afraid of the sunshine. Such people need to be confronted and not placated. Someone needs to stand up and challenge them.

Oh, for a prophetic voice that does not bow to one's friends or seek political influence. We fail morally when we let the power for self-indulgence perpetuate itself.

The Power of the Pocketbook

The late Donald Grey Barnhouse, a mighty Bible expositor, tells about the time he was dining with the officials of an outstanding Bible college. The table conversation turned toward several letters of criticism that had been received from contributors.

One woman wrote to the institute noting that a photograph of some of the students showed they had "short hair." She demanded that the institute justify this shocking lack of "holiness" before receiving any more gifts of support from her.

Another contributor had noted in the student news that there had been a class play. He, too, threatened to withdraw his support. When he was told it was not a play but a dramatic skit presenting the gospel, he wrote thanking them for their explanation and continued his giving.

Ah, the power of the pocketbook, especially when it gets you what you want.

Positions of authority in the church should be granted on the basis of spiritual qualifications and natural abilities — not on the amount of their tithe each month. The fact that a person is related to a certain family or has been a church member for a long time or has given certain amounts of money does not qualify them for a position of leadership.

Some people attempt to dominate a church because their family is a large contributor. The longer they are in control the more they are in command. When certain families demand this right of proprietorship, the body of believers is paralyzed — both spiritually and functionally. Other members are left feeling demoralized by their lack of information or input. Inevitably such a church or organization will eventually wither and die.

Years ago, when I was a pastor, the church desperately needed a new organ. I was thrilled when a family approached me and said they wanted to donate one.

One day, a member of the congregation wanted to use the organ to practice for the Sunday service. When she asked the family for the key to the organ, they wouldn't release it. "Since we gave the organ to the church, we'll decide who plays it," they said.

When I heard about what had happened, I called the family and said, "We would like to keep the key to the organ in the church office so everyone who needs it can have access to the instrument. If, however, you want to have sole control of the key, then you can come and remove the organ from the sanctuary."

They relented and gave up the key.

Pride and Power

In some groups it's not the members but the structure or the leader who pulls the strings.

Perhaps the perceptive writer was accurate when he said that pride is one of the monumental problems of our day. Why? Because pride makes us think we are right, and power gives us the ability to cram our vision of rightness down everyone else's throat.

The sad thing is that institutions, especially religious ones, find it so hard — or almost impossible — to admit they are wrong or to express sorrow when they make a mistake. Their pride, which is actually an unwillingness to admit failure, raises questions about their own integrity.

My friend, Dr. Arthur Parsons, told me about an incident he had to confront when he was the chief denomination official in Ohio. A woman phoned him one day, obviously in distress.

"The minister informed me that next Sunday morning during his sermon, he is going to call me out from the congregation and present me with a baby pacifier," she explained, almost on the verge of tears. "He said if I wanted to be pacified he would accommodate me."

Dr. Parsons couldn't believe that a pastor would put a member of his congregation in such an embarrassing situation.

"What should I do if that happens?" she inquired.

"Accept it, and be seated on the front pew," he responded. "On second thought, send it to me if he gives it to you."

In a few days, Dr. Parsons received the pacifier in the mail. Then he called the pastor and asked him to come to the state headquarters.

When he arrived, Dr. Parsons inquired, "Was there a

time during your sermon last Sunday that you called someone to the platform and presented them with a nicely
wrapped pacifier?"

"No, I did not do that."

Dr. Parsons went to his desk, pulled out the pacifier,
and further questioned, "Have you seen this pacifier before?"

The minister confessed, "Yes, I did do that."

Shortly thereafter, the pastor left the church, and his
abuse ceased. Unfortunately, he was a bitter, wounded man
who never recovered.

Having a mean attitude and lording it over people does
not bring the reward that we seek. In fact, the marriage
between pride and power carries us to the very brink of the
demonic.

In the brilliant book titled, *The Dream Lives On,* Dr.
Rose Sims, who has invested her life working with rural
United Methodist Churches, describes the battles she had
with those in control of her own denomination. She tells how
a single committee could render the most powerful bishop
in America impotent to make appointments or select candidates for the pulpits he was supposed to fill. She writes about
one incident:

> That meeting with the committee had noth-
> ing to do with me or competency, accountability,
> nor even very much with discrimination. It had to
> do with power — power to fill the pulpits of
> Methodism. It had to do with seminaries that turn
> out pastors whose vision is far from Wesley's. It
> had to do with impotent, voiceless laity who have
> been told, and who believe, they have no recourse
> but to pay apportionments and the pastor's salary,
> even if their church is being killed.[1]

One of the great tragedies in today's religious organizations is the deception that goes on behind closed doors by the keepers of the gate. This arrogance manifests itself in so many ways.

Someone observed that Jesus never intended to start a business but to lay the foundation for a closely knit family of people, caring for one another. Has the church become a structure superimposed on the life of the people? Are the people really allowed to be a part of it? Is their role to just support the structure?

Playing God

Super-spiritual people who are on a holiness binge or a "God told me" crusade can wreck havoc within a church body and create confusion for the spiritually immature.

Thirty years ago Donald Grey Barnhouse wrote the following in an editorial:

> One of the most dangerous things within the bounds of Christendom is the tendency of some people to play God for others. They pass over the organized efforts to be God and guide for all people, such as is found in some denominations and in some religious groups, to concentrate on the tendencies found among many Christians. Examine yourself.
>
> Do you have the thought that someone is not quite as good a Christian as yourself because he does not share your opinions on such matters as amusements or cultural practices?

My esteemed friend, Dr. Arthur Parsons, says there are only two churches — you're born into one, and you join the other.

It may come as a shock to learn that God is not a Roman Catholic, a Baptist, a Presbyterian, or a Charismatic. There is one faith, one Lord, one baptism. It is time we got off our throne and let God be the Lord of all. It's a wonderful day in our lives when we stop playing God.

Success or Character?

One day a young pastor told me, "Your generation taught us how to preach, but not how to live. You taught us how to build big churches and be successful pastors, but you didn't tell us what kind of people we're to be."

It's true. We taught success but not character as the foundation. No wonder there has been so much misuse of power by those in positions of authority.

Much of what has been written in the press in the last two decades has made lesser men of us, because we have become power seekers.

What have we learned by the failures of well-known leaders and prominent people who have had to admit immorality? The scandals of the past few years when men of God grabbed for power and sought to retain title and position at any cost should have taught us something.

Unfortunately, the evangelical community has not studied the tragedies that have taken place among us. I would think they would want to try and prevent further embarrassment and to develop a system of checks and balances.

Why hasn't that happened? Because we are all so fearful of disturbing our own nests. We are also fearful of each other. We are scared we will lose some power if we look for the truth.

In the spring of 1987, William Saphire wrote a column in which he discussed the infighting and power plays of the religious wars. He concluded his column by saying, "The greatest lesson of this Gee Whiz Gehad is that each of us — preacher, pollster, pundit, prognosticator, Paul, partisan, or president — risks a fall from grace in a reach for power. After the fall, repent, make restitution, shake hands, and salvation is around the corner."

Unfortunately, it's not as simple as that.

The Purpose of Confrontation

Like the incident with the man who refused to sign the check for his church board, we need to confront those who are misusing their power. The point, however, is to get them to properly use their power and help them realize that what they are doing is wrong. Our motive should not be to expose them publicly or embarrass them.

If our objective is to hurt people, the best way to do that is to get up and publicly ridicule them, which accomplishes nothing. But we can, in a loving way, get involved in their lives and tell them what they are doing is not producing the results that they seek.

I've been in congregational meetings where board members have attacked the pastor in front of those present. Their intention was not to help; their purpose was to humiliate or embarrass him. We should be equally appalled if a pastor publicly and purposely embarrasses a member of his congregation. Such an unloving act should never come from one called to shepherd his flock.

At the same time we sometimes condone a group who will get together and attack, for example, a deacon, pastor, Sunday school teacher, businessman, or a parent who has the misfortune to have failed in some way.

"We Got Our Church Back"

When I was serving as a denominational official, a pastor called me and said, "The board of our church will not comply with the wishes of the congregation who have voted to build a new building."

"What do you mean?" I asked, wondering if this pastor was jokingly trying to present a worst-case scenario to see how I would respond.

After several phone calls and a visit with the board members, it became apparent to me that they were quite serious and would not comply with the wishes of the congregation. I realized this was no laughing matter.

The pastor asked me to intervene in the situation, and I reluctantly agreed.

I arrived at the church and spent an evening with the board members discussing their unwillingness to comply. I quickly realized several of them were seasoned veterans of past political scrimmages in the church. They considered themselves to be the elite members of the congregation who knew what was best for the church.

Having assessed the situation and the personalities involved, I said, "You need to get on with the task at hand and do what you were told to do by the congregation." As far as I was concerned that was the end of the matter.

After several months, however, I was informed that they had not responded and had no intentions of doing so.

Another meeting was planned; this time with the entire congregation in attendance.

I stood before the people and explained what had taken place between myself and the board. Then I said, "The rebellious spirit and attitude exhibited by your church board makes your church body no longer welcome as a member of the denomination."

Shocked, the people silently looked at one another.

"As a congregation, however," I continued, "you will be given an opportunity to vote as to whether or not you want to remain a member of our association of churches. If you vote to remain, a new board must be appointed."

For over an hour, I listened from the pulpit as several hundred people attacked, hissed, and booed me in an open meeting. It grieved my heart to see such conduct displayed in a manner that could hardly be reconciled with the work of the church.

As I watched and waited, I remembered well an evening years before when our state denominational leader and I had spent time with the board of this same church. We had pleaded with the church council to take out a small life insurance policy on their pastor. It was going to cost them approximately five dollars a month to provide a $10,000 policy. I knew the church had the money, but they refused simply because they wanted to play tough and not comply with our request. At the time, we didn't know that the pastor already had cancer. He died shortly after our appeal was rejected.

That incident and others came to my mind as I stood and waited for the congregation to air their views.

Finally, the vote was taken as to whether or not the people wanted their church to remain as part of our denomination. When the results were counted, the congregation had voted to stay within our organization.

Devastated and angry, the power-block that had ruled and dominated the church for years rallied together to decide what to do next. I was still presiding over the meeting when their group, which included about seventy-five people, stomped out the door.

I didn't know what to do next so I just kept quiet. Sensing the congregation's deep pain and sorrow over the event, I began to speak in consolatory hushed tones.

Suddenly, from the center of the church, a little lady stood up and raised her hand. "May I say something?" she asked.

"Of course," I replied.

With a look of peace in her countenance, she simply stated, "It appears we just got our church back!"

Relief swept over the congregation, as everyone realized that the power of the elitist group had been broken. Now for the first time in many years, there would be a shared spiritual commitment to the goals the people wanted.

Full of Grace and Truth

How did Jesus deal with people? He was blunt when He talked to the Pharisees, and they never forgot it.

But, oh how gracious He was with those whom He knew would respond when confronted about their sin.

When He came to the woman at the well in Samaria, instead of saying, as we might have, "Woman, you are an adulteress," He graciously suggested, "Go, call your husband."

His graciousness won her, and her life was changed.

Oh, that we, as His disciples, would learn what it means to be "full of grace and truth."

[1]Dr. Rose Sims, *The Dream Lives On* (San Leandro, CA: Bristol Books, 1989).

9

Christian Power Brokers

You shall have joy, or you shall have power,
said God; you shall not have both.

Ralph Waldo Emerson

The sun set as the private jet eased off the runway. In the small passenger section a conversation was beginning between a nationally known evangelist and a pastor of some prominence.

As the plane eased into the clouds and headed for Washington, DC, the discussion began about the effect that the evangelical church was having on life in America. The conversation focused on the relationship that President Bush was seeking with well-known pastors and other religious people of some repute.

In the midst of the discussion, the pastor said, "I'm very grateful that the president of the United States would ask someone like me to counsel him on matters that he feels are vital to American life."

The evangelist replied, "It's very wise of the president to get advice from people who are well-known and have some influence."

The pastor, obviously sincere, said, "The White House wants to keep this visit private. They don't want a lot of fanfare or press coverage about our advising the president. In fact, I was told to enter the White House through an entrance that is not generally seen by the press."

The evangelist straightened up in his seat, turned toward the pastor and stated, "The only door I'll ever enter at the White House is the front door! If I don't come in the front door, I won't go in any door!"

The pastor, obviously taken aback by the evangelist's display of arrogance, quickly ended the conversation.

Instead of viewing a presidential invitation as an opportunity to serve the country and the president, the high-profile personality had turned it into an occasion for a grand entrance at the White House front door.

This kind of attitude is exactly what people find offensive in leaders — the high-mindedness, the aloofness, the disdain of some power brokers. It's a tragedy whether it's in business, the church, Congress, or whatever realm of life.

I know because I got caught up in it and paid a dear price.

For many years prior, however, I had been able to deal effectively with power. Then I abused it. Now I know that success can be our biggest enemy.

Without power or authority, we have fewer opportunities to abuse it. It's when we are in a position of power and authority that failure often comes. We must never close our minds to temptations, but be constantly on the alert for the abuse of power.

The Privileged Few

Within our society resides an element of people who

are convinced they are right about most things. That means anyone who doesn't agree with them must be wrong. They are imperialists.

Imperial legislators.

Imperial business people.

Imperial educators.

Imperial ministers.

Imperial Christians.

They impose their ideas upon us by pushing their agenda. Their goal is to dominate our minds, our actions, what we believe, and what we should think about ourselves. Because they consider themselves the privileged few, they feel it is their responsibility to make the rules for all of us. They think they should tell "the people" what is best for them. What they really mean is: Follow me, but don't ask any questions.

Sometimes they are in places of leadership. We put them there because we believe them to be servants, but they are not servants at all. They want to be lords — people who desire to control our minds.

You know them. It's the boss who rules with a heavy hand and demands perfection of everyone but himself. It's the congressman who considers his constituents mindless waifs who don't have a clue about how the government should be run.

It's the religious leader who sees his "partners" as unschooled folks unable to discern God's will. Although they consider themselves the evangelical aristocracy, the classical Pentecostal, or the elite Charismatics, they are only deceiving themselves and have lost their sense of servanthood.

Only by hypocrisy, fear, and lies can the privileged few exist. They can survive no other way. When we come into contact with those who regard themselves as the privileged few, we most speak up, speak out, and call them into account. If we acquiesce to people of this mindset, we contribute to their delusion and become victims of their abuse.

Christian Power Brokers

To arrogantly seek power is not a spiritual attribute; it is a sign of selfishness and pride. Anybody who wants to grab power and hold on to it because it gives him prestige is a treacherous person. In an effort to become imperial, he takes on a mentality that says, "I'm enjoying this leadership. I know what is best, just follow me!"

Do some people of power — layman, preacher, businessman, educator, government official, or whoever — enjoy the glitter, honor, and prestige of being a leader? The going to the head of the line, the adulation?

Do they see the people as brothers and sisters, and themselves as one of their fellow servants, or are they more inclined to keep the flock in their place? Do they thunder the message as to what the work should be? Or do they happily lead them like a shepherd?

When a Christian leader becomes a power broker, he denies the cross of Christ.

Our attitudes toward people are often an offense to God and to the ones we are striving to serve. While people are often desperate for leadership — godly, inspired leadership — we are holed up in our "work". When that happens, we can easily become insensitive to how people feel.

It is a dangerous thing when you become your own boss. You grow immune to any criticism or counsel or to the feelings of other people. Those who follow the leadership of the greatest Man who ever lived should bear one another's burdens. That trait, however, seems to be at the bottom of the list among some people of power.

Demanding, through our own resources and power that things be done the way we perceive God wants them to be done, is not the answer.

Many of us who have spent time in prison are drawn to

the works of Dietrich Bonhoeffer. My dear friend, John Anderson, a true brother in Christ with whom I shared many precious moments in prison, gave me one of my most cherished volumes. Bonhoeffer spells out so clearly in his book, *Life Together,* what I needed to hear:

> He who loves his dream of a community more than the Christian community itself becomes a destroyer of the latter even though his personal intention may be even so honest and earnest and sacrificial.
>
> God hates visionary dreaming; it makes the dreamer proud and pretentious. The man who fashions a visionary idea of a community demands that it be realized by God, by others, and by himself. He enters the community of Christians with his demands. He sets up his own law, and judges the brethren and God himself accordingly. He stands adamant in a living reproach to all others in the circle of brethren.
>
> He acts as if he is the center of the Christian community, and as if his dream binds men together. When things do not go his way, he calls the effort a failure. When his ideal picture is destroyed, he sees the community going to smash. So he becomes first an accuser of his brother, then an accuser of God, and finally a despairing accuser of himself.[1]

We see that happening time after time. A man sets himself up as "God's man," and forges ahead, forcing everyone behind him to fall into line or get out. Then when everything tumbles down around his ears, the accusations come from every direction — especially from within.

True Friends

I have tried the way of recognition, honors, and exaltation. It is all vanity, and it demands a heavy price. At PTL we were obsessed with this lifestyle of vanity, and all it brought us was pain. I went astray by attaching myself to a dream.

One night, not long after my release from prison, I was sitting alone in a hotel in Cincinnati, Ohio, feeling very forsaken. My pain resulted from my longing to see and know the fellowship of friends with whom I had worked for so many years. As I remembered the wonderful times we had shared in the past, I realized how much I missed my former colleagues. We had shared visions and dreams, but now I was alone.

When I failed in the place of power, I also failed others — people who had stood by my side and been a part of my life. As long as I held an important office, these friends sought my companionship. But they vanished when my title and position were stripped from me.

It is difficult, I admit, to know how to minister to and accept one whose conduct we cannot approve or condone. I understood the reason for my former colleagues' reluctance to associate with me, but that didn't make the pain any less.

Today I hurt for those lost relationships, but I know they will probably never again be restored. Some of my former colleagues, people in whom I had invested my time and life, are on their way up the ladder as ministers and businessmen. Now they don't need me anymore.

That is probably good. Now I look "to a friend who is closer than a brother."

It makes me wonder if their identification with me in the past was based solely on my position of power. Today, with a record as a convicted felon and no longer in a place of leadership, I can't do anything for them.

When my world tumbled around me and the network satellite trucks were camped at the end of our driveway and helicopters were flying over our house, a dear man and his wife came to see us.

This brother didn't come for an interview or to get the latest scoop. He came to deliver a message.

At the time, I was the object of a national scandal and the laughingstock of the media. *Who would want to be associated with me now?* I wondered. During the years that I was a denominational official, he was the superintendent of our churches in Ohio, and we were close friends.

Like the Good Samaritan, it took great courage for a man of his stature and reputation to push past the media and pick me up as I lay wounded by the side of the road. As soon as he saw me, he said, "I'm here, and I will not let go of you. I will walk with you whatever happens. Don't be afraid. I'm going to be there with you."

Later, when the scorn, the ridicule, and the accusations came, I wondered if he would desert me like so many others already had. But he still stood by my side. For people to get to me, they had to go through him. He put himself between me and the world and simply said, "I'll walk with you."

While I was in prison and it seemed all was lost, this dear brother didn't forsake me. In fact, he drew closer to my wife and me, seeking only service and not the accolades of others.

For the past five years, he has been my friend and mentor, and I have submitted myself to him and his leadership. Today, Dr. Arthur Parsons is the chairman of the board of our ministry, Life Challenge. He has proven to be a true friend and brother.

Falsely Accused

During my fourteen years on my denomination's highest elected body, I saw the limits men and women would go to achieve power. As they clawed their way to the top, at times I was appalled by their tactics and what they will do to hurt and destroy anyone who got in their way. I learned a lot about myself and others during that period of my life.

I remember one incident as if it were yesterday.

As we walked down the street in Denver, Colorado, a group of our church executives were returning to the Civic Auditorium after lunch for the afternoon session of our bi-annual general conference.

One of the executives turned to several of us and stated, "Are you aware that our denominational leader is the chairman of the board of a local bank in Springfield, Missouri?"

It was apparent from the tone of his voice that this was more than an attempt to inform us of the appointment of one of our leaders to the position in the bank.

James E. Hamill, one of our church's most respected leaders, replied with a smile, "They sure couldn't find a more qualified man."

I quickly responded, "It's none of my business who the chairman of a bank's board is."

Then the accusing executive began to spew out of his mouth all of the negative factors that he could possibly bring to light about the situation. At the time, he seemed to be the only one interested in discussing this topic.

After a few months, this non-story and trumped up charges were made public by syndicated columnist, Jack Anderson. It soon took on a life of its own and captured the attention of the national media. Stunned by this sudden interest, the general board of our denomination was brought together from throughout the United States, and our highest elected body looked into the matter.

I was appointed to chair a committee to investigate the accusations. The deeper we looked into the matter, the more we could see that our denominational leader was being falsely accused. It was evident that someone who was seeking power for himself and his work was encouraging the investigation. He had been challenged by leadership and did not like it, and so he sought revenge.

For almost a year, our denomination was preoccupied with a situation that should never have been in question. In the end, our committee found nothing to indicate inappropriate behavior or conflict of interest on the part of the accused leader.

The one who had leaked the story to the press and had broken covenants of confidentiality had walked away from it all without ever being confronted with his deception. We should have exposed the person involved. In my opinion we owed the one accused and his family, our deepest apologies for failing to stop this abuse of power by a jealous person seeking to overthrow our leader.

Power was the real issue, and my heart broke to see it raise its ugly head in a place where it should never occur — within the church. That was my first experience with such a blatant abuse of authority, but it was not my last.

Christian Double-Dealing

Conflicts of interest abound in Christendom, and most lay people would be shocked to know what goes on behind the scenes of some institutions and religious organizations.

I call it "Christian double-dealing." It's the mental gymnastics that leads those in positions of authority to think anything they do is okay as long as it's for "the greater good." Does that concept, however, only mask their true intentions? Many times decisions are made to appear as those best for all concerned when, in fact, they are made to benefit the decision-makers — either to boost their reputations or feather their nests.

Those in high places proclaim fairness and uprightness, and they want people to be accountable to them. But when the tables are turned, and they are confronted with their own dirty tricks, they cry, "Foul!" and refuse to play the game by the rules they devised.

My most disappointing moments in the past five years have not been those times when secular or government officials were meting out judgment against me. Their laws clearly defined their actions, and they acted, in most cases, with professionalism and courtesy.

Some of my deepest hurts have come when, in my dealings with religious organizations, I was tried, convicted, and sentenced without the Bible ever being used as a guide. What grieved me most was that at no time was a scriptural approach used.

Not once in the past five years since the collapse of PTL has any leader suggested to me that we should resolve our differences by following a biblical pattern. Over and over again, I have raised the question, "Why don't we use the Bible to resolve this problem?

I think I know the reason. Many religious power brokers see themselves as part of a giant Christian conglomerate. Their focus is on the business of the organization and its management and success. As a result, scriptural processes are never spoken of, thought about, or carried out. The agenda of the group goes forward with only lip service paid to the teachings of Scripture.

My late dear friend, the Rev. W. T. H. Richards of Great Britain, said to me, "Why do you Americans have constitutions and by-laws for your churches in America?"

I quickly responded, "So we can explain to our people what we believe and how we should conduct ourselves."

He looked at me quizzically with a pained expression and responded, "Do you Americans really believe that you can explain the Bible better than the Bible can explain itself?"

I have thought much about that statement.

When I was a boy, one of the things stamped into my mind by my beloved pastor was the truth of the Scriptures. We were taught that the Bible was sufficient for matters of faith, doctrine, and relationships. It was often said, "If anyone believes that you need a supplement book equal to the Scriptures, then you are on shaky ground."

A pastor who is not of my denomination remarked to me one day, "Our church manual states in its introduction that the Scriptures shall be the guide for all matters of doctrine, conduct, procedure, and discipline." Then with pain in his voice, he said, "You know, that's the last time the Bible is mentioned."

Servants Not Strutters

The best safeguard against the abuse of power is to remember the teachings of Jesus. We are servants, not masters of anything. We are shepherds, not bosses. We are workers, not executives. We have but one Master, one Lord, one King. He is the great "I am."

Let us get off our thrones and put the crown of thorns on our heads. We are to decrease; He is to increase. We are not citizens of this world; we are strangers and aliens!

We are not landlords but sojourners of another country. We have no home here. We are redeemed — not by corruptible things such as silver or gold, but by the precious blood of Christ. There should never be any strutting in His presence — none!

In *The Dream Lives On,* Dr. Rose Sims, writes, "The world is sick at heart about a power that struts. It is hungry for a power that serves."[2]

Let us cease our arrogant strutting and bend our knees to Him who is worthy. Let us bow, not strut. Submission is the gift of ourselves that brings healing. It is the act that brings reconciliation. Not strutting!

I heard a discussion recently by some Catholic clergymen. One of the leaders raised the question, "Who is the most influential person in the Roman Catholic Church?"

Someone responded, "Well, it certainly isn't the pope. It's Mother Teresa."

Although she is the most respected, influential person in the Catholic Church and possibly the entire world, Mother Teresa doesn't even own a decent pair of shoes. What makes her so compassionate and selfless?

The answer is easy: She has a servant's heart. Without

raising her voice she is an example to the whole world.

Where is our love for people? Whether it is in the White House, the office, the factory, the parsonage, the base commander's office, the classroom, or the kitchen — where is our love for the people we serve?

Every person should — with some regularity — write the names, events, and results of the people they have personally helped during a set period of time. The results should come, not from letters or phone calls, but from holding the hands of the bereaved and embracing the lonely.

When someone calls, are we quick to respond? Or do we insulate ourselves from human needs? Are we unreachable, living under the security of unlisted phone numbers and obscure post office boxes?

Jesus was not like that. We who follow the lowly Nazarene must not be offensively insulated and isolate ourselves. Let us come down off our perch and wash one another's feet.

[1]Dietrich Bonhoeffer, *Life Together* (San Francisco, CA: Harper San Francisco, 1992).
[2]Dr. Rose Sims, *The Dream Lives On* (San Leandro, CA: Bristol Books, 1989).

10

The Power to Be Yourself

Power at its best is love implementing the demands of justice. Justice at its best is love correcting everything that stands against love.
Martin Luther King, Jr.

I grew up on an Illinois farm during the heart of the depression. My father worked for the WPA (Roosevelt's Work Project Administration) and brought home $12.00 a week to a wife and five children.

Our few cows and a railroad track composed the setting for much of my young life. Many evenings I would go to my favorite place on a gentle sloping hill that overlooked both our pastures and watch the trains pass by. In the dark, I could see the lights inside the Pullman cars and the people who were bound for distant places — places I had only read about in books.

As I sat there in the twilight hours, I knew we were poor

compared to the passengers on the trains. At times it seemed impossible that God could unlock the dream He kept burning inside me. As early as six years old, I knew God wanted me to serve Him.

Although I have traveled all over the world many times since then, and, in spite of the fact that I have held high positions in life, many times I am still the little boy who sat on the Illinois hillside watching the trains go by, feeling very unworthy.

The person who attempts to grab power is often sending a message that they feel inadequate. But you don't get power by your grip. God has a better way to fulfill your desires.

When all is said and done, only God can make something out of nothing. Still, he chooses to use human instruments, so it is up to us to become the best we can possibly be.

The enemy of our souls enjoys heaping unworthiness upon us. He especially targets people who are committed to the Almighty and to one another.

Our Lord, however, draws us to a higher plain.

> That ye may walk worthy of the Lord unto all pleasing, being fruitful in every good work, and increasing in the knowledge of God;
> Strengthen with all might, according to his glorious power, unto all patience and longsuffering with joyfulness;
> Giving thanks unto the Father, which hath made us meet to be partakers of the inheritance of the saints in light:
> Who hath delivered us from the power of darkness, and hath translated us into the kingdom of his dear Son (Col. 1:10-13).

God has made His redeemed children worthy through

Jesus Christ. We must be of great worth if the Father cared enough to send His Son as our sacrifice.

Many Christians, however, are brought up to "poor mouth" themselves. We need to reverse these negative images of ourselves and train our minds to accept all that the Holy Spirit desires for us.

Submitted power, properly used, should be our goal. To truly love ourselves, we must be willing to follow some of the basic steps of life.

Love Yourself

Most of us have read and re-read the phrase from the Gospel according to St. Matthew, "Thou shalt love thy neighbor as thyself" (19:19). We repeat the words piously in church, and we invoke the need to be concerned about others.

Jesus, however, also makes it clear in that verse you are to love yourself! He readily accepted self-love and did not rebuke it.

How you love yourself reveals how you will love your family, associates, and neighbors.

Loving yourself brings into focus your uniqueness. Think of it: Millions of souls have never been — and will never again be — duplicated exactly. You are an original, fashioned precisely the way God designed you.

Because I have learned some valuable lessons in life and want to flee from power and all of its accompaniments, I am having to re-learn the art of loving myself as God desires. Let me share some principles I have gleaned about loving myself as the person that I am.

1. Learn to establish your presence.

It's possible to do this without brashness or conceit when we know God has a specific plan for our lives.

The apostle Paul is a good example. When the Apostle arrived on the scene, people knew that a man who walked with God was in their presence. Yet he did so by being himself with his security firm in Christ.

As a young man, I had the privilege of having lunch with Ernest S. Williams, a revered man who had been the top executive and spiritual leader of our denomination for more than two decades. I was struck with awe at this ninety-year-old minister. For me he seemed to be the father of our church.

During our meal, I tried to ask him some questions that were important to me. "What are your priorities in life? What was important to you years before that is no longer important today?" I wanted to learn from him.

Finally, after several questions, this righteous man stopped his eating, looked directly into my eyes, and said, "Just do it like I did, and you'll end up all right."

There was more truth in that statement than I realized at the time.

It was the same kind of wise confidence that led Paul to write, "Follow me as I follow Christ." He wasn't attempting to push himself forward, he was just being himself.

2. Believe you are God's person.

If we have been called to a task, the Lord must know that we are capable. Do it with gusto, not with a weary feeling of duty!

If you know God has called and assigned you to a particular job, you can be content without trying to force your way up the ladder.

I became a Christian as a boy. When Oral Roberts preached in my home church in Granite City, Illinois, I walked forward and knelt at an altar. For me it was a symbol of surrender, of giving my life to Christ. I had only one desire: to be a Christian.

As I began to walk with the Lord, I prayed, read my Bible, and participated in the activities of the church. After joining the youth program, I wanted to become a leader in the group. Then, as a young man, I thought it would be wonderful if I could be trained as a pastor. After attending college, I was offered my first pastorate.

Then I prayed, "Lord, if I just had the opportunity to be a leader of a group of churches. . . ." Then I became an area leader. Then I wanted to be a missionary. While serving in Belgium, I hoped to be appointed an officer over an area of our denomination in Europe, and I was.

I wanted to be president of a Bible school, and I was.

That was not sufficient, and I said, "Lord, if I could be a person of some authority on the state level to manage the business affairs of our denomination. . . ." Then that opportunity came. But it was not enough.

I said, "Lord, if I could have the power to be the state superintendent as a bishop in the church . . . ." And I was.

"Oh, God, that I would be a leader on the national level of our church . . . ." And I was.

And on and on it went until God gave me the opportunity to touch not only my community and my state but the world through the ministry of PTL. Until it all came crashing down.

The day came when I bumped into God and came back to the prayer I prayed as a young person: "Oh, God, that I could just be a Christian." I wanted nothing more!

The point of this is what the prophet said: "All is vanity and vexation of spirit." After you've got it all, what have you? Nothing. That's the bottom line.

Too often we move away from the simplicity that is in Christ to things that are totally unrelated to the spiritual part of our lives.

There are more of us who are power seekers on power drives than we care to admit.

3. Know that God's kind of success is available to those who desire His best!

Whether it is winning a contract, teaching a class, a

notable achievement, a promotion, or giving a speech, we must realize our full potential. Don't accept less!

Success must be linked to effectiveness. That is the real measure of success — that we are doing our job successfully, but also effectively. To get the most out of what we do, we must want to do it and be willing to pay the price to achieve the best.

4. Contribute something!

View yourself as being able to do something for people, for the Kingdom, or for the company where you work. Have a servant's heart.

Not long ago, a friend came to me and said, "You will always be a leader to me, whether or not you hold any office."

"Why is that?" I asked him.

"Because when you were my bishop and I was under your leadership, we knew you loved us." His words meant a great deal to me.

I had considered myself a mentor, a leader, a counselor, a friend to these dear people — not because of my official title or elected position — but because of the relationships that had been formed. As a result, my love was unquestioned.

Because of the associations I had developed with people over the years, I received letters from church officers — while I was in prison — asking for my recommendation for men being considered as pastoral candidates.

5. Accept full responsibility for being what you are.

Don't alibi! We all have problems in our backgrounds, hurts in our pasts, and "skeletons in our closets," but our Lord is the Master Forgiver and Healer of our hurts. We cannot wallow in the past forever!

6. Strive for the best, but don't be a hypocrite!

Learn from those around you, but don't try to imitate them. Be yourself as you are spiritually directed.

Early in my ministry, my beloved Aunt Marie kept me on course by listening to me and leveling with me. Long ago, after I took my first pastorate, I invited her to come and teach a series of messages in the church I was pastoring.

I was thrilled to offer such a great opportunity to my aunt, but most of all I was glad she would see me in action! I put on quite a show when she arrived, leading the people in worship and waxing eloquent.

When the service was over, and I knew I had "wowed" both the church and my visitor, we sat down for a snack. Aunt Marie looked across the table and said, "Richard, what's your problem?"

"Problem?"

"I'll tell you," she continued. "You're living closer to the people than you are to God."

I was stunned! But instantly I knew she was right. She touched my soul with her candid words: "When you live close to God, He rubs off on you. It shows up in your conversation and in everything you do. But when you live closer to your people, you soon begin reflecting their value system."

"What should I do?"

"You must walk close enough to God," she counseled, "that these people can see Him in you. Then they will want more of Him."

7. Study people who are leaders and learn from them.

Read the great biographies about men and women who were effective leaders — achievers who kept a balanced view of themselves. Study the things that people have done, what they said, what they wrote. Open your mind to a dimension of their thinking.

Ask yourself questions like: What does Billy Graham

teach about God's love and mercy? What kind of life does he lead? His biography reveals the life of a committed and dedicated man.

I recently read an enlightening article about Billy and Ruth Graham's son, Franklin. His life and works are a testimony of God's faithfulness to his parents. Franklin Graham is an unusual, hardworking, and dedicated person who gives himself to helping others.

Study the life of Mother Teresa. You'll learn what it means to serve others who can give you nothing in return.

Mark and Hulda Buntain, missionaries to India, are two of my personal heroes. For nearly half a century, they gave their lives totally to God and the people of Calcutta. Even since Mark's death, Hulda carries on the work of feeding and educating the needy children of Calcutta.

8. Develop a passion for excellence.

Most people are followers, not leaders. And few people become great leaders.

Doug Kingsritter played for a championship football team in high school and college and was an All American tight end. He later played in the National Football League. After being with the Minnesota Vikings and several Super Bowl teams, he was asked, "What's the difference between the coaching in high school, college, and the professionals?"

He thought a moment then replied, "The coaches in high school and college probably know as much, but Coach Bud Grant sees *everything* that happens when the Vikings are playing. He never misses a thing."

A great leader single-mindedly focuses on the area of his concern and becomes an expert through study, discipline, and experience.

9. Be disciplined — in body, soul, and spirit.

We must bring ourselves to the discipline of denying ourselves. Let us do without things we hold dear to us.

Take care of your body. Work hard, sleep well, and eat what you need, not what you want. Before you eat, ask yourself, *Is this what I need, or is it what I want?*

Exercise! No one else can do it for you.

Life must be disciplined. How we live and feel tells much about how we discipline ourselves. I have had to come face to face with this issue.

Keep asking yourself, *Why am I doing this?* I will be judged eternally for all things. We must nurture our souls. Be quiet. Listen to your heart. Don't close it down. Do what is right! Tell the truth. Live in private like you do in public. Let your soul feed on things that are wholesome.

Keep a good attitude! Stay sweet! Don't fight, you will never win! Rest in God! Maintain a quiet and gentle spirit.

Keep your mind under discipline. What is going on in your mind? Remember, evil begins in the imagination. Keep your mind pure. Evil may drive by your mind, but don't give it a parking place.

10. Keep it simple.

Have a livable lifestyle. Don't compete with your neighbors. Don't get in debt beyond your ability to pay it back comfortably. Share with others God's goodness to you!

Be content with what God has given you. He knows how much you can handle.

Pray this prayer: "O Lord . . . keep falsehood and lies far from me; give me neither poverty nor riches, but give me only my daily bread. Otherwise, I may have too much and disown you and say, 'Who is the Lord?'" (Prov. 30:7-9).

King Solomon knew the danger of having too much money, but like many others, he failed to follow his own advice.

This illustration from the book, *Windows*, reveals the worthlessness of material possessions if our hearts are not right with God.

The eighty-two page inventory of Elvis Presley's estate, totaling $10,000,000, included a complete inventory of his mansion, Graceland. The house was filled with statues of tigers, lions, elephants, dogs, birds, a ram, a whale, an eagle, and a dolphin. Elvis collected statuettes of Joan of Arch and Venus de Milo, one of which came complete with an electric waterfall.

For transportation he had two Stutz Blackhawks, valued at $100,000 each, a Ferrari, a Cadillac, an International Harvester Scout, a Jeep, a Ford Bronco, a custom-built Chevy pickup, three tractors, seven motorcycles, seven golf carts, three mobile homes, and six horses.

He had eighteen TV sets, including two seventeen-inch color sets installed in the ceiling above his nine-foot-square bed. His wardrobe consisted of one hundred pairs of trousers, twenty-one capes, three cartons of shoes, and three jewel-studded vests.

His trophy room was decorated with his army discharge papers, forty-one plaques, thirty-two photo albums of his films, and thirty script albums, plus scrapbooks and trophies from fans, record companies, and karate clubs.

His musical instruments included seven guitars, one of which had his name inlaid in mother-of-pearl.

"For what shall it profit a man, if he shall gain the whole world, and lose his own soul?" (Mark 8:36).[1]

11. Don't be a prima donna and don't be pompous.
We need to remove the elitist spirit out of our hearts. Let's put our telephone numbers back in the directory. Let us be disturbed during our meals. During our days off,

let the telephone calls come. Let us be awakened in the middle of the night for hurting, needy people. Let us be needed in our moments of rest by sobbing souls yearning to speak to us.

12. Tell the truth, only and always!

When you deceive, you are the most deceived.

There is a vast difference between a confidence and a secret. A secret is something known only to us. A confidence is something we share in confidence with a confidential relationship. It will never be told.

If you don't have the ability to hold a confidence, you shouldn't make others believe you can be trusted. People ask, "Will you keep this a secret? Can I talk to you in confidence?"

If you are not going to do that, don't lie. Be honest and say, "No, I can't do it."

13. Don't talk about yourself all the time.

Be interested in others! Your projects and plans are very important, but so are those of other people! Learn to listen.

All the great men I have known were genuinely interested in others. Those who only spoke of themselves, however, often failed.

14. Don't quit!

It is a sin to do less than your best. Keep at a task until it is finished. Never, never, never give up. You will win, probably because you endured. Stick to the job.

Do not accept defeat easily. Keep moving forward. Your Creator will help you to create answers to your problems and needs. God's creative genius is yours for the asking.

How to Meet Life

Unfortunately, any feelings of unworthiness you may have are often compounded when problems arise. You need to learn how to meet life's turbulence and ups and downs.

Though He was perfection incarnate, our Lord faced a less than perfect world.

The apostle Paul, a man of human frailty like ourselves, also met many triumphs and tragedies. None of us are exempt from the difficulties and problems of life.

When you face struggles, what can you do?

My friend Alan Groff suggests we have five alternatives:

1. You can *run!* Some people do this a lot, but they almost always land in another batch of problems.

2. You can *ride it out*. Sometimes you can't solve every problem, but like the rodeo cowboys you may have to hang on, endure the rough going, and see what happens.

3. You can *break up the problem*. If you can't handle a situation, sometimes it's best to segment it. Like the tired joke — How do you eat an elephant? One bite at a time!

4. You can *share it*. Everyone needs a confessor, a sounding board — often a spouse or unquestioning friend.

5. You can *give it back*. Some things we just cannot take. There will be times when you will not be able to carry everyone else's burdens. We must know our limitations and not condemn ourselves because we cannot be everyone's savior — your place is to point them toward the true One who can.

Blessed is the person who has skin with the proper

thickness — who can work happily and confidently despite enemies *and* friends.

We get from people what we give. We find in them what we bring. We discover that the changes in them are really changes in ourselves.

Do you feel unworthy to be a person who can be used to help humanity? Join the ranks!

> And God also selected [deliberately chose] what in the world is lowborn and insignificant and branded and treated with contempt, even the things that are nothing, that He might depose and bring to nothing the things that are.
>
> So that no mortal man should [have pretense for glorying and] boast in the presence of God (1 Cor. 1:28-29;AMP).

Our loving Lord will give us the power to love ourselves.

[1]R.L. Whitworth, *Windows* (Green Forest, AR: New Leaf Press, 1988), p. 29-30.

11

For Better or Worse

Since all of us can wield power through our unique abilities, all of us are subject to the temptation of abusing power. Fathers abuse children, and husbands and wives will abuse their spouse, whether it is verbal or physical abuse. Some exercise power with the information and knowledge they possess. Others have power through their ability to speak persuasively.

Wesley Pippert

Statistically, one out of every two children will grow up in a home torn apart by divorce. That figure is the same for Christians.

Some marriages function by power rather than by relationship, and the consequences can be disastrous. The abuse of power in a marital relationship normally centers around money, sex, and work. It is in these areas where things can go awry and abusive spousal power takes hold.

Marriage, more than any other relationship, certainly offers the potential for conflict. In every area of life we have opportunities for disagreement, but living together and seeing each other at our best and worst moments brings our true nature to light.

Sometimes husbands and wives openly express negative feelings with intensity, and at other times we withhold personal expectations from each other. Seldom, however, are marriage partners negotiating the continual changes that life brings at the same pace or at the same time.

Only the husband and wife who have had a genuine salvation experience will be best able to withstand the sexual, financial, emotional, and spiritual onslaughts ahead of them. At present there are powerful forces drawing husbands, wives, and children in opposite directions.

The Power Struggle

Many broken or rocky marriages can be traced back to two common failures.

1. Misuse of power.
2. Mistrust.

No couple marries with the intention or desire to destroy their relationship from within, but this far too often becomes the case.

The first common erosion occurs when either one or both members in the marriage have a strong need to be right — all of the time — in every situation. As one who often counsels with couples in broken marriages, I often refer to this as the "my way or the highway" syndrome.

Instead of relaxing into the truth that ideas, opinions, approaches, and behaviors can be different, and also acceptable, many couples wrestle with "right or wrong," "better or worse," "win or lose," and ultimately "who is in control."

Conflicts often arise over insignificant things like meal times, entertainment choices, bed times, driving habits, etc. Then these tiny erosions begin to touch the more tender places as the husband and wife start guarding their turf and protecting their ground. Soon a tug-of-war develops, and someone always loses even though no one wins.

As the power struggle escalates and the stakes of the game get higher and the tactics more hurtful, the common battlegrounds become sex, money, and the kids.

Often at this point in the Christian home, the scriptural mudslinging will start with angry challenges of:

"You're not submitting to me as a godly woman."

"You do not love me as Christ loves the Church."

"Your body is not your own."

"You're not fulfilling your priestly duties in the home."

I long for the occasion when some hurting, bleeding person will walk into my office and ask for help expressing his or her failures and spiritual insensitivities instead of reciting frustrations with the spouse!

We know, but we often forget, that when we only know another's failure, we haven't learned much. It is when we see ourselves as we are, with our inconsistencies and misdeeds, that we can truly be helped.

Power Statements

The need to be right — the need to have the power — slowly chokes out the early characteristics of trust and service to one another. As a result, the couple who started as the same team finds themselves at the opposite ends of the field, trying to out-maneuver, over-power, or win by any method. Winning in these situations means defeating their mate, and victory comes through power — power misused, power abused!

Let's look at some of the power statements we often make in an effort to control our spouse and the situation at hand.

1. "I'm right you're wrong! And I don't need to hear what you have to say."

The one in pursuit of spousal power always avoids

being wrong at any cost. Being right achieves dominance over the other partner and puts the abusive spouse in control. The possibility of equality is nonexistent in this kind of relationship. Being wrong is unacceptable, so they make their spouse responsible for any mistakes that occur.

The spouse being controlled, however, usually becomes angry, and a power struggle develops. As a result, the partners are more concerned with control than with the quality of their marriage. This compulsion to know the right and wrong way guides their lives.

2. "It is your problem."

This kind of condescending attitude reflects selfishness in its highest form.

How often have we heard the phrase, "If only you would have listened to me, this would not have happened." That statement is used to relieve ourselves of any responsibility and point fingers at the other spouse.

3. "You should anticipate my desires and my feelings."

When that statement is made, the response is usually, "Why do we have to discuss it?"

Before long someone is screaming, "You know what it takes, and what you must give to make me happy and fulfilled!"

All of these statements reveal the underlying problem in most marriages: self-centeredness. That is certainly one of the signs of fatal conceit.

Ten Ways to Destroy a Marriage

Here are ten ways that fatal conceit can lead to spousal power abuse and destroy a marriage.

1. Soliciting and demanding personal attention.

One spouse may tend to monopolize the relationship,

ask for special attention, parade his or her accomplishments, and keep others waiting in order to maintain a sense of control. The person seeking control will constantly demand approval, and the central point of the discussion must be him or her.

Personal growth in the other partner is thus inhibited. As a result, a distancing from each other usually occurs in the relationship.

2. Bossing or punishing.

This is accomplished by manipulating the other spouse, controlling by lecture, talking down, finding fault, blaming, critiquing, and ridiculing. The advantage belongs to the attacker, so they soon learn it is important to strike first. As a result, the one taking the initiative accuses the other of responsibility for whatever is perceived as a mistake. This type of spousal power places the responding partner in a defensive position and makes him or her vulnerable to manipulation by the attacker.

3. Withholding intimacy.

Often a spouse who desires power will create and maintain a distance from his partner. To do this, the husband or wife will withhold genuine intimate involvement in the relationship for fear it will compromise his or her superficial power base. If that happens, the abusive spouse will no longer be able to control the partner. This kind of abuse often forces the forsaken partner to find warmth, acceptance, and friendship from others.

4. No giving, only getting.

"What's in it for me?" is the question on this spouse's mind. Sometimes the "getter" will use charm, wit, persuasion, disapproval, or displeasure to get what he or she wants from others. An uncooperative, manipulative, quest to use the other spouse for selfish gain can destroy the self-esteem of the one being abused.

If one spouse constantly needs to receive, the other has to constantly give. If one only believes in logic, the other has to suppress the need to express feelings. If one insists on dominating, the other assumes a subdued role.

5. Seeking to be in control.

Those who are fearful that life will control them often turn the tables to make sure they control others. The "controller" becomes a master at withholding his or her feelings from the other spouse by intellectualizing to avoid showing emotion. This spouse deprives the relationship of spontaneity in an effort to maintain their image as the partner in control. As a result, the priority is to control himself, the partner, and the relationship. Spontaneity is gone, and the love ceases. The fulfillment never arrives, and trouble is on the way.

6. Presenting an image of righteousness.

Sadly, some spouses think that their goodness will bring them fulfillment, joy, peace, and happiness in the marriage relationship. That's why they feel compelled to point out the weaknesses of others. The wrangling in this kind of relationship is characterized by a selfishness that regards only his or her own personal feelings and opinions. The other partner becomes discouraged. Because the abused spouse is never good enough, he or she begins to assume the role of the "bad" one in the relationship.

7. Being superior.

The priority here is to be better than others. Sadly, this attitude reflects itself most often in Christians. In reality, the "superior" spouse often feels inadequate or unequal to his or her mate. As a result, the abusive spouse over-compensates by pretending to be more competent, more effective, more recognized, and more useful than the other spouse.

As a result, the other partner shuts down on risk taking and sharing in the marriage, fearing that whatever is said will be heard in a different way than intended. The weaker partner becomes pressured, submissive, controlled, manipulated, and cautious to avoid an oversensitive reaction from the "superior" one.

8. Exacting vengeance.

When a mate feels unloved or betrayed with no hope of ever being accepted, he or she often seeks revenge. This discouraged partner may resort to hurting the other spouse by word or by deed in order to even the ledger.

Believe me, some people do keep the books and records in their minds about their marriage relationship. As a result, vengeance becomes an obsession, leaving the other spouse at a decisive disadvantage.

9. Expecting too much.

When things aren't going well in a marriage, there can be a threat of rejection that can lead to discouragement on the part of the victimized spouse. This tactic of power continually expects the partner to be more and more, and do more and more to keep the power spouse happy. The weaker partner begins to realize that no matter what they accomplish, it will not meet the standards set by the mate. Unrealistic expectations can intimidate the other spouse to the point where he or she feels incapable of ever being acceptable.

10. Withholding affirmation and acknowledgment.

When we fail to recognize progress and give positive feedback to the one we love the most, we deprive our partner of the motivation that they need to keep excelling. Holding your mate's hand or giving a gentle, loving hug will accomplish wonders and help him or her to excel. The spontaneity of a kiss on a cheek or a loving passionate embrace can produce the best and affirm more than we even anticipate in our marriage.

A Better Way

Now that we've identified some of the attitudes and actions that can damage the marriage relationship, let's look at some ways to strengthen it.

One of the best ways is through positive communication. Remember, there is a language of love. Too often, however, we forget the need for heart to heart communication in our marriage and family relationships. How sad when we move from a couple in a dimly lit cafe, smiling and whispering special "nothings," to stoic people who stare blankly at each other with little to say and less in common.

Remember the "Alley Oop" cartoons? The men always used a handy club to get the women's attention. Or do you recall the old comic strip "Maggie and Jiggs?" Maggie got her points across to Jiggs by whacking him over his bald head with a well-placed rolling pin, by red-faced yelling, or by slamming him against the nearest wall! We could resort to such methods, but there must be a better way.

John Powell, in his book *Why Am I Afraid to Tell You Who I Am?* lists five levels of communication:

1. Cliché Conversation
"Honey, I'm home. How are you?"
"Fine. How was your day at the office?"
"It was okay. How did things go with you today?"
"Fine. Dinner is almost ready. Can you call the kids?"

2. Fact Reporting
"Oh, by the way, before the children come in from outside, perhaps I should mention that Joey got two failing grades on his report card."
"Two F's, huh?"

3. Idea and Judgment Expression

"Yes, two! And I think it's about time that you do something about it."

"Me? You're home with Joey in the afternoon."

4. Feeling and Emotion Expression

"Are you saying that our children's education is MY responsibility?"

"No, but I feel that you could do a lot more to help Joey with his homework."

5. Deep Personal Communication

"Honey, I don't think you realize how frustrated I am when I have to face the same after-school problems day after day. I really need you and your wisdom to help handle some of these situations.

"I have been putting a lot on you, but a lot of it has to do with all the extra activities and responsibilities I've taken. I think we need to talk more about this after dinner."[1]

Communication, especially on the deepest level, requires honesty, courage, and acceptance. Happy marriages and open family relationships are rarely the product of chance. Instead, they must be designed intelligently and deliberately built.

Communication, deep and true, is possible. Indeed, it is necessary, because no Christian's ministry is stronger than his marriage or family relationships.

A good communicator eliminates the negative — nagging, criticizing — and emphasizes the positives — giving honest appreciation, paying attention to loving details, being courteous, and establishing openness.

Grow Up!

A survey involving 100,000 couples revealed a startling concept: Passionate love lasts an average of two years.

If the husband and wife were not good friends by the end of those two years, their marriage eventually died, whether by divorce or by neglect.

Passionate love does not have to fade away. Numerous couples in their seventies, eighties, and nineties attest to an ever-present passion. However, there must be more than passion for a marriage and family to stand together through the years.

The key is maturity. That is the trait of good marriage partners. Maturity involves accepting some things as they are, constructively changing other trends, and having common, worthy goals for improvement.

What characterizes a mature marriage partner? The following is paraphrased from Leonard Wedel's *Maturity I.Q. Check-up:*

1. A mature person never takes himself too seriously. He is serious about his relationship with God, his spouse, his family, his work, and his fellow man, but he realizes that he is always fallible and never indispensable.

2. A mature person strives for spiritual, mental, and physical health.

3. A mature person does not always view with alarm every adverse situation that arises.

4. A mature person is too big to be little or petty.

5. A mature person has faith in himself as he becomes stronger and more fortified through an intensifying faith in God.

6. A mature person never feels too great to do the little things and never too proud to do the humble things.

7. A mature person never accepts success or failure, in him or others, as permanent.

8. A mature person never accepts any moods,

in himself or others, as permanent.

9. A mature person is one who is able to control his impulses, especially when lack of control may hurt the ones he loves most.

10. A mature person is not afraid to make or admit mistakes, nor is he unwilling to accept the mistakes made by others.[2]

The sad truth is this: We are all young once, but we can choose to stay immature forever!

Love and Understanding

Unselfish love is another characteristic of a good marriage. Love helps us to be aware of others' needs and moves us to meet those desires. The best interests of our mate must be placed first in our hearts and minds. Our interests must be second.

That sort of love keeps the marriage warm even through sickness or disappointment. Christian leaders, whose ministries are so closely tied to their families, must exhibit extraordinary amounts of love and understanding.

Saint Francis of Assisi, the thirteenth century leader, wrote the following lines which should be required reading for every Christian, especially those involved in family relationships:

Lord, make me an instrument of Thy peace!
Where there is hatred, let me sow love,
Where there is injury, pardon,
Where there is doubt, faith,
Where there is despair, hope,
Where there is darkness, light,
Where there is sadness, joy.
O Divine Master, grant that I may not so much seek
To be consoled, as to console,
To be understood, as to understand,

To be loved, as to love.
For it is in giving that we receive;
It is in pardoning that we are pardoned;
It is in dying that we are born to eternal life.

Families who live in spiritual "glass houses" are especially susceptible to the forces that would pull relationships apart at the seams. Love makes the difference — quiet understanding, mutual confidence, sharing, forgiving, and loyalty through both good and bad times.

"Love," according to Ann Landers, "is the day in and day out chronicle of irritations, problems, compromises, small disappointments, big victories, and working toward common goals." Well said!

Christians who discover the necessity of love and understand it will realize that the results make up for the tension, lack, hurt, and discouragement along the way.

[1] John Powell, *Why Am I Afraid to Tell You Who I Am?* (Allen, TX: Tabor Publishing, 1989).
[2] Leonard Wedel, *Church Staff Administration: Practical Approaches* (Nashville, TN: Broadman Press, 1978).

12

The Power to Parent

The choice you are making (as leaders in your home) is obvious. Your home will be a place of devotion or division, authority or anarchy, camaraderie or confusion, spirituality or sensuality.

Lowell Lundstrom

In America, we receive more instruction about how to drive a car than we do about how to be a good parent. As a result, the haphazard, sloppy, dangerous effects of poor parenting are reflected in the lives of many children today. As a nation, we are dismayed, shocked, and saddened by the tragic consequences.

Sure, training is lacking. But what training do parents lack? What don't they know? Or if they know, what don't they do? When do parents find themselves off track?

As Christians, we can turn to the Scriptures for advice on how to be good parents.

And now a word to you parents. Don't keep

on scolding and nagging your children, making them angry and resentful. Rather, bring them up with the loving, discipline the Lord himself approves, with suggestions and godly advice (Eph. 6:4;LB).

Too frequently parents operate from a position of power over the child rather than responsibility toward their child. They chasten but frequently fail to instruct.

They invest their money but not their time. When they do take time it is for recreation or pleasure, so that they can "enjoy" their children and be amused by them, completely ignoring the responsibility for training.

The responsibility of the parents is to impart their laws and commandments in loving, consistent, repetitive manner so that the children are trained in behaviors and attitudes. (See Prov. 22:6.)

A child is often expected to behave in ways he was never trained to behave! Fathers will say, "Any twelve-year-old should know how to mow a yard and wash a car." They ridicule their children's abilities when they have never trained their children in these supposed simple tasks. Parents abuse power when they refuse to invest the time necessary to instruct the child.

As a result, anger toward the parent swells in the heart of the child. He recognizes his failures in the attitudes of his parents, and he becomes discouraged. (See Col. 3:21.) We misuse our God-given authority over our children when we fail to guide and instruct.

Proverbs 6:20-23 speaks of children not forgetting their father's commandments nor forsaking the laws of their mother.

> Young man, obey your father and your mother. Take to heart all of their advice; keeping in mind everything they tell you. Every day and

all night long their counsel will lead you and save you from harm; when you wake up in the morning, let their instructions guide you into the new day. For their advice is a beam of light directed into the dark corners of your mind to warn you of danger and to give you a good life (LB).

The lamp and the light of the mother and father are necessary and important foundation stones in preparing the child to be awakened spiritually. A child, who has learned through living instruction from his parents, can then boldly step into the lamp and light of leadership of his own family. The Word has been hidden in his heart, and the Holy Spirit can direct him.

Fathers and Mothers

Each member of a family has a role in the core unit.

The man brings his own masculine viewpoint into the relationship. In a well-constructed family, the father is a "court of appeals." He is accorded a certain authority and a heroic quality.

The Bible clearly distinguishes between men who fulfilled and those who failed in their parental responsibilities. Abraham was told that his generations would become a great and mighty nation because he oversaw and trained his household in an effective, loving manner. Eli, on the other hand, lost his prestige and priesthood because "his sons made themselves vile and he restrained them not."

The apostle Paul realized the need for involved fathers and wrote Timothy that the office of bishop or deacon should only be conferred upon the man "that ruleth well his own house."

Cheney, in his *Job of Being a Dad,* and Stearns, in *The Challenge of Youth,* both placed much of the blame for the breakdown of the modern family unit upon the failure of fathers to function properly. Too often it seems, fathers take their responsibilities with little seriousness, bestowing both parental functions upon his wife.

Any father who has a correct and proper parental conception of the family unit and an adequate appreciation of the tremendous parental responsibilities, will put his home at the center of his priorities. All other interests other than his relationship with God will become subordinate. The father's influence upon the lives of his wife and children is a responsibility that no other institution or government can ever assume.

Likewise, the mother brings an invaluable set of resources into the family unit. And to her children, there are no words to describe a good mother's value. President Abraham Lincoln agreed, "All that I am or hope to be I owe to my mother."

During the most impressionable years of life, the mother should be the child's most accessible teacher, and from her the child acquires much of his moral and spiritual nature. The very presence and example of a godly mother constantly brings an elevating influence to the home. Righteousness, from the beginning of a child's life, does not come by nature, but by example and practice. And because of the enduring results of early character building, a mother's contribution to the home increases by multiplied proportions.

Children, who are molded by sentiments, opinions, beliefs, and moral standards, learn first by imitation, then by comprehension. The Christian leader's home, therefore, should be the "greenhouse" where tender lives are shielded and shaped during those most impressionable years. It should be a child's inalienable right to be loved, understood, educated, and trained in God's ways. It is in the home that children should first receive positive, enduring concepts of God's love.

Obviously, marriage and child-rearing are integral parts of a very serious whole. Such responsibilities should be approached soberly by the Christian leaders, with much effectual prayer, and in daily communion with the Heavenly Father.

Making a Difference in a Child's Life

The child's view of God, their concept of self, and their ability to relate effectively to others is dramatically impacted by parental relationships.

What a difference it makes for the child when someone believes in him. When he has felt loved and been supported in a system built on true relationships, the child's life is characterized by security and self-confidence.

On the other hand, the family that has been characterized by harshness, demands, and abuse leaves any child with a feeling of inadequacy and a sense of not being able or capable of pleasing others. Such feelings of insecurity may lead to a lifetime of withdrawal from others caused by a defensiveness that prevents the child from engaging in true, meaningful relationships with others.

These negative traits were often seen in the inmates I met in prison. Let's face it, people have big problems in their lives when they have not known the confidence and affirmation of others. The way a parent relates to the child determines whether the child will be kind or harsh, loving or aloof, attracted or ambivalent, trusting or suspicious, complimenting or criticizing in his or her relationships to others.

In the inconsistent atmosphere of inadequate modeling, children really don't know what to expect of others, or what is expected of them. We must communicate to our child that we value them as a person. This will give them a great sense of security in their own being.

The Absent Parent Syndrome

Our children need our time, attention, love, support, and our affirmations. We are commanded not to provoke our children to anger (Eph. 6:4). Neglect and abandonment, whether emotional or physical, and a misuse of our power, are the stimuli that provoke anger.

One specialist dealing exclusively with addictive and destructive behavior stated that 99 percent of the people he worked with came from homes where there was an absent or a bad father. The deception revolves around the usage of "bad" or "absent".

A parent would tend to say, "I'm in the home; therefore I am not absent. I must be okay." Others say, "I'm not a person who batters, and I don't beat my children; therefore I am not a bad parent. I must be okay."

Abusive parental power has as much to do with omission as it does commission. It's not always what we actually commit that determines abuse. What we withhold can be equally destructive.

Parenting is about getting involved; it's about being a parent. When a mother or father is absent from the family, he or she forfeits the enjoyment of developing a relationship with the child. Regardless of the reason for the absence, it deprives children of the time and emotional support they need.

When parents are seduced by the power of success, they typically withdraw from their children in the pursuit of other activities. The relentless search for success, whose purpose lies in having power, accolades, and notoriety in the career and social sector, has serious consequences. This type of physical and emotional abandonment can leave a child with an inability to trust others and a sense of aloneness and insecurity.

I have often seen these characteristics in children of people involved in Christian ministry or in other high commitment, twenty-four hour a day work. When parents have to work 50 or 60 hours a week and are deeply involved in numerous outside activities, the child reaches out for some place in that schedule. Although the motives and purpose behind our work may be noble and pure, it doesn't matter, especially to the child who feels he is being neglected. He simply wants time with the two people he loves the most.

When we reject, or fail to respond to a child who is crying out for our touch and for the security of our presence, we deprive him of one of the more important components of love — simply being there.

Children need a time of focused attention from their parents. That is the key. Time, in and of itself, is not necessary. It's more than that. It is focused attention, where for that period of time the child knows that someone loves and someone cares. Nothing takes the place of focused attention; there is no substitute for that intimate time. When we fail to give it, we are hurting ourselves and our children who are helpless in the situation.

Emotional Abandonment

These days, parents often feel overwhelmed by the pressures of life. A child, however, doesn't really see things that way. To them it is abandonment.

Emotionally withholding ourselves from our child creates damage that generally persists throughout his or her life. If a child is being rejected, or when there is an emotional disengagement by a parent, the child will try to protect himself from being hurt and abandoned again. To do that, he will back away from any type of intimacy in relationships.

When we as parents emotionally distance ourselves from our child, it makes it difficult for the child to receive love from anyone — especially God. If they could not win the love and acceptance of their parents, then how could they accept the love of another at face value? The abandonment of children reflects a fatal conceit that can bring great hurt to many.

Power without relationship is emotional abandonment. Emotional abandonment leaves the child susceptible to all the vices of peer pressure. In his search for fulfillment, which has been lost through the absence of parental relationship, a child can easily be deceived or seduced by worldly influences. If the child doesn't gain the relational intimacy he requires with parents, they are prime targets to be exploited by self-serving people who identify this need in their lives.

Children deserve quality time with each parent to validate their personal importance and worth. Exclusive time spent with each child is vital. When it isn't present in a parent/child relationship, it communicates that he isn't significant or of value to God.

Parenting by Intimidation

When a parent fails to build a relationship with the child, the result is generally a power play that attempts to over-control the child. Intimidation is the best definition of this phenomenon. Predicated on a rule of dominance with no affirmation, this kind of overbearing parenting can drain the life and creativity out of a young life. It can also lead to other forms of abuse.

Let's look at three ways this can happen.

1. Perfectionistic parental standards

Perfectionistic parents set standards so high and rigid that even they cannot achieve them. If they can't, neither can their children. As a result, the child is left with the feeling of never being able to measure up in the parent's eyes.

Perfectionism differs from encouraging the child to excel and glean rewards in life. Instead, it pushes the child over the emotional edge.

This type of manipulative and controlling power will result in one of two things. The child will desperately try to "measure up" but will internalize hurt and anger because of the impossibility of attaining unrealistic expectations. Or the child will simply rebel and withdraw. He will seek out peers who do not succeed and bond with them. Why? Because they are failures and don't represent a threat to the child.

Cultivating perfectionism and demanding it of your child creates a subtle form of abuse of parental power. It is a fatal conceit.

2. Withholding verbal affirmation from our children.

A spoken message of kindness and trust, affection, and affirmation is important. "We believe in you, we trust you, we love you. You're doing a great job. We appreciate you." Those are the kinds of statements our children should be hearing.

Criticism and condemnation are destructive. It takes twenty positive messages to overcome every negative one. Abuse of power totally reverses the order and makes any accolade merely unheard. In this kind of negative environment, a rejecting atmosphere is produced and a spirit of hopelessness develops in the child.

When we don't recognize children as the gift and blessing of God — as God's heritage — we abuse our power as parents.

3. Denying a child security and safety.

Parental power takes on a devious and diabolical form when it justifies physically abusing a child. Almost every day newspapers report some form of child abuse being perpetrated by power-hungry parents. In today's world, children are often abused, not by the parent but by their mother or father's live-in partner.

Recently, a twenty-seven-year-old man, living with a woman, held her child by his ankles and dropped his head into the toilet bowl and drowned him. Why? Because the child was crying. This should rankle our spirits and send shock waves through our hearts.

Children have the unequivocal right to expect physical safety in the presence of their parents. Anything less than this is a moral, ethical, spiritual, and legal issue. Any parent who puts welts and scars on children should be prosecuted as criminals. It is the most exaggerated form, along with sexual abuse, of a violation of parental power.

A young lady, her life in shambles, sought counseling in an effort to sort our her tragic past. Through tears, she told the counselor how her father had sexually abused her since she was about twelve years old. The abuse had continued throughout her teenage years, until one day her father threw her out of the house.

Why did he throw her out? Because she had painted her fingernails with polish.

In her father's mind, wearing nail polish was a sin. His set of power rules were of his own making, and when his daughter crossed the imaginary line, he discarded her.

Some people have strong convictions, yet they don't have purity of life themselves. They are totally blind to the sin in their own lives.

Taking the Lead

A Christian home can be many things: a lighthouse, a playground, a workshop, a forum, an intimate restaurant, a health resort, a business enterprise, a haven of refuge, and — most of all — a temple of worship.

Paul wrote that a Christian leader should rule well his own house (which in the Greek means "to stand before, to lead"), "having his children in subjection with all gravity; for if a man know not how to rule his own house, how shall he take care of the church of God?" (1 Tim. 3:45, KJV).

A Christian home, by definition, should be built around Christ. A Christian leader reveals much about himself by the way he leads his Christ-centered home.

In his insightful book, *Heaven's Answer for the Home,* Lowell Lundstrom wrote:

The choice you are making (as leaders in your home) is obvious. Your home will be a place of devotion or division, authority or anarchy, camaraderie or confusion, spirituality or sensuality. In the surveys we have conducted among Christians in the Midwest, only one in ten families has family devotions together. This is one reason why so many Christian families are having trouble, why so many churches lack the spirit of revival, and why so many pastors are discouraged because they see no spiritual progress in the families of the church.[1]

What should be done? First, except in households where the husband is absent, the responsibility of spiritual authority belongs to the man. Throughout the Bible this was true of strong families.

Secondly, he should set aside a regular time for the family to get together for brief Bible study, prayer, and worship. Most problems reveal a spiritual need and require spiritual solutions. By action and words, the husband and father must say, "I am accepting my God-given role as head of this household. As head, I rebuke Satan and his influence from my wife and family. I plead the blood of Jesus over each of us, and I proclaim that Jesus is Lord over this home!"

Lastly, he should make sure that the family attends church together. It is up to the father to see that the spiritual needs of his family members are met.

Security, significance, and worth come exclusively from God, and Him alone. When we do not effectively model the character of God to our children, we abuse our power as parents.

We must pass on to our offspring that our purpose in life is to eminently glorify and honor our Saviour. Nothing should be more important than that. A child picks up what is lived out before him — that's what he will remember best and most.

> Believe in and on the Lord Jesus Christ — that is, give yourself up to Him, take yourself out of your own keeping and entrust yourself into His keeping, and you will be saved; (and this applies both to) you and your household as well (Acts 16:31;AMP).

If ethical standards, integrity, and a lifestyle that pleases God is lived out in the home, the chances are much greater that the child's aspiration will be to have the same kind of a fulfilled life. His actions will follow the thoughts and beliefs of his parents.

[1]Lowell Lundstrom, *Heaven's Answer for the Home* (Springdale, PA: Whitaker House).

13

The Safety of Submission

I have never been so pleased, as when I could shift power from my own, on the shoulders of others; nor have I ever been able to conceive how any rational being could propose happiness to himself from the exercise of power over others.

Thomas Jefferson

Again and again Sam Walton confounded the skeptics who awaited his demise. Impossible, they said, to maintain a discount store in a town of less than 50,000. He not only proved them wrong but contradicted Wall Street when they predicted his homey, small-town philosophy couldn't sustain a $10 billion business.

The Wal-Mart chain, based in the small town of Bentonville, Arkansas, today boasts over 1,500 retail stores and adds 150 more each year, making it the largest retail operation in the world. Before his death in 1992, the company

Sam Walton built had passed the $50 billion mark with no signs of slowing.

In *Sam Walton: Made in America,* by Sam Walton with John Huey, the small town entrepreneur spells out his rules for building a business. Of particular interest are rules 2 and 5:

> Rule 2: SHARE your profits with all your associates, and treat them as partners. In turn, they will treat you as a partner, and together you will all perform beyond your wildest expectations.
>
> Rule 5: APPRECIATE everything your associates do for the business. A paycheck and a stock option will buy one kind of loyalty. But all of us like to be told how much somebody appreciates what we do for them. We like to hear it often, and especially when we have done something we're really proud of. Nothing else can quite substitute for a few well-chosen, well-timed, sincere words of praise. They're absolutely free — and worth a fortune.[1]

That's why Wal-Mart employees are called "associates" and made part owners of the company.

In 1985, Walton was chagrined when *Forbes* magazine disclosed he was the richest man in America. The revelation invited unwanted news coverage and requests for interviews.

"We're not ashamed of having money," Sam confessed, "but I don't believe a big showy lifestyle is appropriate for anywhere, least of all here in Bentonville where folks work hard for their money and where we all know that every one puts on their trousers one leg at a time. . . . I still can't believe it was news that I get my hair cut at the barber shop. Where else would I get it cut? Why do I drive a pickup truck? What am I supposed to haul my dogs around in, a Rolls-Royce?"[2]

Sam Walton lived comfortably but modestly. He was married to one woman and devoted to his children. He loved his country and went to church.

Billy Graham called Sam Walton, "one of the most remarkable Americans of this century. The simplicity of lifestyle, the deep religious commitment, and the overwhelming success in business, all make him a role model for all America."

His love for people showed in the way he provided opportunities for them, and together they wrote one of the great success stories of American history. Walton knew how to choose managers and how and when to delegate authority.

The whole nation rose up to honor him on March 17, 1992, when President and Mrs. George Bush flew to Bentonville to present Sam M. Walton with the Presidential Medal of Freedom. Sam said it was the greatest day of his life.

Sam Walton understood *who* owned the store, and he never forgot it.

Never Own Anything

Years ago A.W. Tozer wrote an essay titled, "Five Vows to Spiritual Power."

One of the vows was: *never own anything.* "It is not wrong to acquire things," Tozer wrote, "it is not wrong to own a home or car, or to earn a degree, but it is detrimental to your spiritual life to own anything in the sense of not turning it over to God as first claimant."

It is tragic in every area of human life to forget that we are servants, not lords; stewards, not owners. This is not my church or my business in a possessive sense. I don't own the store. Even my life is not my own. I have been bought with a price.

The longer you have the job, the title, the position, the more you think you are entitled to it, which leads you to take liberties you otherwise would not take. I call it a supposed "Right of Proprietorship." When we begin to act it out, it can be deadly!

As Charles Wilson, former president of General Motors, said, "What's good for General Motors is good for America."

So we begin to say, "What's good for me is good for my family, my church, my business;" and when we do that, we're prone to want all the accompaniments and accouterments of power.

It's easy to start thinking, "This organization can't make it without me." When you do that, you begin to believe, "I own this airplane, this equipment, these supplies, this money, this business, or this company."

When you feel you are the owner instead of a steward, you become self-protective and possessive. Then you start to sow discord among others in order to protect your own turf. When that happens, you are headed for trouble.

Power is such an alluring, deceptive, inviting thing that before long you are doing things you would never have permitted before.

Very few people start out with the mentality "I'm going to become a crook today," but through subtle little compromises, they start down the slippery slope.

Leadership is Not Forever

Why do you think American corporations have defined retirement dates for their executives? Because they know if the leadership is not submitted to an overall plan, the thrust of what they are doing will not work over the long haul. Success will be a temporary, fleeting thing at best.

It's important to remember that leadership is not forever. There are no exceptions to that rule.

It's tragic when the founder of an organization, the person who started the business, the long-time leader of a school, a denominational leader, or the pastor who started the church believes that his vision is greater than the institution. It's dangerous when a person has power, and the man thinks he's the only one who can accomplish the work.

Fulfilled is the pastor who can serve a congregation with a conviction that he is God's man for the job. Nobody can do it better than he while he is there. But when his time is up — be it a year or five years or thirty years — and he leaves, he knows God will find someone to come in and shepherd that flock. The same is true of the politician, educator, businessman, or chief executive of any organization.

Let me give you an illustration of proper stewardship.

An airline pilot has the authority to enter the cockpit of an aircraft. He is qualified by skill, training, and experience to fly. He has the temperament and has passed the physical examination.

Together with the navigator, co-pilot, and attendants, he will fly that aircraft from, say, Chicago to Los Angeles. When he arrives in Los Angeles, he will leave that plane, knowing that the next person has the competence, experience, and skill to handle the job as well as he.

While he was sitting in the pilot's seat, he had the authority to fly that airplane, but he did not own it. It was not his — it belonged to the airline. And when he arrived at the destination, he left the aircraft for somebody else to fly.

That's how we should use the authority God gives us — whether it is as a businessman, pastor, manager, steelworker, superintendent, carpenter, coach, executive of a large corporation, or in some other position of trust and responsibility.

What is Submission?

While I was at PTL, I should have raised questions about the lifetime partnerships that eventually led to our downfall. I should have insisted or should have myself disclosed the number of partnerships that we were offering to the public.

Those of us who took the blame can alibi and develop rationales about what we did, but I know in my own heart where we went wrong. We found it difficult, if not impossible, to submit ourselves to others who did not agree with our way of doing things.

A number of people told us what we didn't want to hear, but we refused to listen. That was our greatest sin.

There is safety in submission. But I learned that lesson too late.

What is submission? Submission is the willingness to turn loose. A strong leader must be willing to submit. Politicians, CEOs, and business people should praise it. Ministers *must* have it.

The submissive leader says, "I don't have to be in charge. I am committed to the point where I can turn loose of the authority. I will submit myself and what I do to others."

Submission is self-imposed. We don't do it for our own sake.

Why is submission so important in the life of the believer? Because it protects us from the innate evil nature lurking within ourselves.

Michael Palmer, a professor at Evangel College in Springfield, Missouri, listed some of the values in submitting to others:

1. Submission is God's way of protecting us from the unfavorable results of our own worst judgment.

Every person has a blind side, especially as it affects things about us — our families, our work, our lives. That's why submission and accountability to one another is so important.

In today's world, people — whether they be taxpayers, church members, or consumers — expect those at the top to respond to them. Some people who aspire to power don't understand this. They are out of touch with what has taken place in America in the last ten years.

Those in places of leadership — congressmen, presidents, news reporters, non-profit organizations, pastors — are being held to a higher standard of accountability by the public. It's no longer a free ride to the top, and without submission it can be a quick trip to the bottom.

A submissive leader is willing to take counsel, to listen to others, and to receive advice. Nobody thinks of everything. We are never so right as when we say, "I don't know."

In my first book, *Integrity,* I made this statement: "We should be more concerned with what people under our authority are saying than the people over us. The true sign of submission is in submitting to those under us, not to those over us, because those who are under us are dealing with more reality sometimes than those who are over us."

If we don't receive any input from others, we only have ourselves to agree with and no one to disagree with us. That's a dangerous place to be.

Sometimes people of power want to submit, but they don't know how. We do them no favors by agreeing with everything they want to do. A kind but firm question or awakening is the best thing that could happen to them.

2. Submission is the way of keeping order in a business, a home, or in a church.

Power people find it hard to admit they can't do it all. They are like the senior pilot of a two-pilot airplane, who says, "I'm going to fly it or else, even if I can't operate all the controls. I'm going to do it myself because I'm the pilot. Come what may, I'm going to fly this plane whether or not someone else flies it with me."

We are all responsible to somebody. If there is no submission, then chaos is the result.

Peter Drucker said, "The man who stresses his downward authority is a subordinate, no matter how exalted his title and rank, but the man who focuses on contributing or serving, and who takes responsibility for results or leading, no matter how junior, is in the most literal sense top management."

The truly strong man shares power. It is an indication of strength, not weakness, when we submit to other people.

3. Submission is God's way of completing the work of making us free.

Submission is a tempering process. When a willing person undergoes this process, it releases him from the tyranny of passions and self-centered motives.

I've had the privilege of preaching at Dr. Yonggi Cho's church in Korea a number of times. Several years ago when the church's membership numbered about 600,000, I preached there on a Sunday and about 25,000 were present.

The next day, Mildred and I went to the airport to begin our flight back to the United States. It so happened that Dr. Cho, who travels extensively, was flying out at the same time and booked on the same plane.

Dr. Cho, whose church is the largest in the world, is a monumental presence in Seoul, Korea. He is well-known by everyone in the country and treated like a dignitary wherever he goes. When he arrived at the airport accompanied by his wife, his mother-in-law — who was a very powerful person in the church in those days — his deacons, government officials, and his chief aide, the airport almost came to a standstill.

As my wife and I filed past Dr. Cho's entourage — a procession of over eighty people — we greeted each one and bade them farewell. It was a heady moment for me to be associated with this nationally-known figure.

Just as we boarded the plane, Mildred leaned over and whispered in my ear, "Honey, remember next Sunday you're preaching in Pocahontas." My mind quickly shifted to our next engagement — a small church in the little Illinois town of about 600, where I would preach to about fifty people.

My wife was reminding me to keep my perspective.

One of the best safeguards against high-mindedness is a spouse or friend who knows our weaknesses and isn't afraid to confront us — gently, of course.

It is said that when Julius Caesar rode past the throngs in his chariot, an aide continuously whispered in his ear, "Remember, Caesar, you're just a man."

Grabbing for Power

People who seek power often put on an act of humility, pretending they don't want a certain office or position, when, in fact, it's written all over their faces. We need to be wary of individuals — and of ourselves — when power for the sake of power is sought. Although it is not wrong to desire a leadership position, we should make sure our motives are pure and our hearts are right first.

Jesus said, "Whosoever will be chief among you, let him be your servant" (Matt. 20:27).

We all know people who have risen to high positions and then became intoxicated with power. Soon they see themselves as some kind of civil ruler over the serfs of Christendom. The real danger occurs when leaders like this refuse to submit to others. Then, a deception takes hold of their leadership, causing them to demean those in authority under them.

Jesus never taught or tried to be a big shot among the disciples. We need to remember what Jesus did the night before He died: He washed the disciples feet.

Leslie Weatherhead, an English pastor whose church was destroyed by Nazi bombs during World War II, wrote:

> When I am hot and rebellious, bitter and
> cynical and sarcastic, when it seems evil can win
> in the world and the battle is strong, when it seems
> as though pride possesses all the high places and
> greatness belongs to those who can grab the most,

when it seems that faith is mocked and humility is trodden in the dust, when pity seems weakness and sympathy, folly, when a foul egotism rises up within me bidding me assert myself, serve my own interests and look out for number one, then, my God, as I listen down the corridor of the years as I listen for the voice of the Almighty, may I hear the gentle splashing of water in a basin and see the Son of God washing the disciple's feet.

In other words, don't grab for power. That's the message. If you receive a place of leadership as a gift from God, you will probably handle it cautiously. But if you have to achieve a certain position by manipulation and scheming and cajolery — by your own work or merit, or by rolling over people — you are tromping in dangerous territory.

I heard David Shibley say, "Ministry received will ultimately succeed, even if it appears for a moment to have failed. Ministry achieved will ultimately fail, even if it appears for the moment to have succeeded."

You don't have to step on people to get where you're going in God's plan.

The Danger of Isolation

Organizations that maintain a rigid top-down management style often lose touch with the common man. It happens so subtly.

The leader in government, business, education, or in a Christian ministry who sits in his ivory office building and surrounds himself only with executive-types eventually becomes isolated. As a result, he begins to view the world much differently from the man on the mailing list who struggles day by day with life's problems.

As the organization grows, the challenge to remain sensitive to the needs of the people becomes infinitely greater. Layers of leadership and perks eventually build walls around executives and leaders, breeding superiority and disdain for those considered beneath them.

It happened to me, and it happens to others. When church leaders — or other in positions of authority — become rich and powerful, they become oblivious to the hurts and suffering of others.

The grip of arrogance becomes so tight, they believe they will go on forever — that nothing can topple them from their throne of power. Swollen with arrogance and complacency, their bloated egos send them on a crash course with disaster.

They forget it is God who calls, anoints, and lifts His people up and puts them down. "Pride goeth before destruction, and an haughty spirit before a fall" (Prov. 16:18).

In his book, *The Velvet Brick,* Howard Butt writes:

> Morality begins at the top. Moral leaders produce moral organizations. Immoral organizations come from leaders who are immoral. Nazi parties come from Adolph Hitler. Your only alternative to organizational tyranny is the organizational God. Father means leader. Son means follower. Since the Father and the Son are indivisible we worship one God, not three. You can't split authority and submission. You cannot think of God except as a servant. Authority and submission interlock constantly. They interact flexibly.[3]

We who are in positions of leadership, in and out of church work — and that includes all of us — must come to terms with the fact that authority and submission go hand in hand.

The Crown of Submission

The Old Testament provides a contrast in leadership styles: Saul pictures rebellion; David embodies submission.

Two kings, two crowns, two styles — one exalted, one extinct.

King Saul is discarded and forgotten in history's dust bin, but 3,000 years later, David is still making headlines. We still call Jerusalem the "City of David," the city of the king.

Rebellion reflects insecurity. When we submit, however, we emit a sure sense of calm and strength.

Howard Butt also writes, "The crown of your Christian leadership is a crown of shining thorns. The crown of revolution disintegrates. The crown of submission is exalted."

No wonder the Bible says of Jesus, "Wherefore God also hath highly exalted him, and given him a name which is above every name" (Phil. 2:9).

Why did God give Jesus this name? Because He humbled himself.

What keeps us from submission? The age-old problem of pride.

Again Howard Butt writes, "My problem is I don't want to be little, like man. I rebel to be big, like God." [4]

The king of all sins is pride. No other sin runs a close second. Beside pride or self-conceit, all other vices — drunkenness, sex sins, greed, temper, violence — are gnats' eyebrows compared to the mountain of pride.

Pride is the sin that made the devil into the enemy of God. Satan refused to be under God; he wanted to lead himself. John Milton described it in *Paradise Lost:* "Satan decided it was better to reign in hell than to serve in heaven."

Pride makes you independent of God, and independence is the diametric opposite of worship. That's why we must submit ourselves to God and resist the devil.

[1]Sam Walton with John Huey, *Sam Walton: Made in America* (New York, NY: Doubleday, 1992), p. 247.
[2]Ibid., p. 8.
[3]Howard Butt, *The Velvet Brick*
[4]Ibid.

14

Choosing the Lesser Place

This is the way of the Christian. He should choose the lesser place until God extrudes him into a position of more responsibility and authority.

Francis Schaeffer

I must admit that something in my character doesn't really want to accept a lowly place. I want to look good. I want to come across well, and I enjoy recognition. So I must guard against a proud look. To some degree, those feelings are true for all of us.

There were times in the past when I considered myself to be *the* man! I thought I had brought mighty blessings upon churches and certain areas of ministry. I was successful. People's lives were transformed. I was loved, appreciated, and received a lot of recognition. I thought I was it!

At ministerial conventions, on television, or in the pulpit, I loved being on the platform. I had a big head and a proud look. I wanted to be used. I desired to be recognized.

When I didn't get the recognition that I thought I should receive, I became irritable and cross. I cared more about what other people thought than I did about my own personal commitment to God. If I was asked to do lesser tasks, I sometimes became upset. I could hide it, but I was still annoyed.

God saw that proud look and dealt very severely with me. Now I find myself being grateful to do anything of service.

I have been broken and shaken. I have seen my proud heart, and it is an ugly thing to behold. No wonder God hates it.

The Proud Look

God despises pride; we all know that. But the writer of Proverbs tells us that He despises a proud *look*! No reference is made to pride in and of itself.

> These six things doth the Lord hate: yea, seven are an abomination unto him: A proud look
> . . . (Prov. 16:17).

What is this proud look that God hates? It's a pharisaical hypocrisy. It is like the man in the gospels who got up and prayed, "Oh, I thank God that I'm not like other men." It is an arrogant self-righteousness that looks down at people and despises them.

"I make large contributions to charitable organizations; I give to the church; I go to church; I pray." It's a constant *I do*. The focus is on "me," and we go about with a know-it-all attitude, looking with disdain at others. *And God sees it.*

God also knows how to deal with the proud look, doesn't He?

When King Herod made a speech on one occasion, the

people heralded his address and rousingly proclaimed, "This is the voice of a god, not a man."

Did Herod tell the people to be still and deny their worship? No, he grasped the adulation. Basking in the roar of the crowd, he gazed over that vast audience. It was a proud look. *And God saw it.*

> Immediately, because Herod did not give praise to God, an angel of the Lord struck him down, and he was eaten by worms and died (Acts 12:23; NIV).

When Moses had married a Cushite woman, his sister let him know she didn't like the choice he had made. With Aaron as her accomplice, they began to discredit Moses to the people.

With a proud look, Miriam proclaimed, "Has the Lord spoken only through Moses? . . . Hasn't he also spoken through us?" *And God saw it.*

> Then the Lord came down in a pillar of cloud; he stood at the entrance to the Tent and summoned Aaron and Miriam. . . . The anger of the Lord burned against them, and he left them. When the cloud lifted from above the Tent, there stood Miriam — leprous, like snow (Num. 12:5,9-10;NIV).

When David made his journey with the ark of the covenant and danced before the Lord, his wife Michael looked through the lattice window and despised him in her heart with a proud look. She was angry and jealous, and coveted David's glory.

God saw her proud look and she "had no child unto the day of her death" (2 Sam. 6:23).

God's response to a proud look is harsh. That's why I

aspire to constantly remind myself and to raise the question, "Who am I to have a proud look about anything?"

I am much safer when I see myself as a fallen prisoner, crying out for God's help and strength and wisdom, than as an author being interviewed on a national television show or signing books at a popular bookstore.

To lift ourselves up above anybody else is an abomination to God. In our lowliness of mind, we must "esteem others better than ourselves."

Suffering the pain, humiliation, and the anguish of being part of a national disgrace wiped the proud look off my face. The shame of bringing reproach to my Lord, my family, my church, and myself left me no room to boast. There can be no strutting in God's presence.

If you have even the hint of a proud look, deal quickly with yourself before God brings you down. A proud look will not prevail.

Spiritual Pride

When someone or a group indicates, directly or indirectly, "We're more spiritual; we have gifts you don't know anything about; we have more power than you," this is a stench in God's nostrils.

We speak of the power of the Holy Spirit, and rightly so, for in Him resides the power behind the gifts of the Spirit. Yet when He bestows a particular gift that person sometimes acts as if it were his to use for his own benefit. That is spiritual pride in its worst form.

A judgmental attitude is another sign of spiritual pride, but it often arrives cloaked in religious-sounding phrases an a legalistic attitude.

Jonathan Edwards, the Puritan masterful declarer of truth, said,

> Spiritual pride in its own nature is so secret
> that it is not so well discerned by immediate

intuition on the thing itself, as by the effects and fruits of it. Spiritual pride disposes to speak of other persons' sins . . . with bitterness, laughter and levity, and an air of contempt. Whereas pure Christian humility rather disposes, either to be silent about them, or to speak of them with grief and pity. . . .

It has been the manner in some places, or at least the manner of some persons, to speak of almost everything that they see amiss in others, in the most harsh, severe and terrible language. It is frequent with them to say of others opinions, or conduct, or advice . . . that they are from the devil, or hell . . . . And they look upon it as a virtue and high attainment thus to behave themselves.

"Oh," they say, "we must be plain-hearted and bold for Christ, we must declare war against sin wherever we see it. We must not mince the matter in the cause of God and when speaking for Christ."

. . . But the imminently humble Christian has so much to do at home, and sees so much evil in his own heart, and is so concerned about it, that he is not apt to be very busy with other persons' hearts; he complains most of himself, and complains of his own coldness and lowness in grace. (Jonathan Edwards, 1703-1758)

During the days of PTL's troubles, I must admit, we were more taken up with Jimmy Swaggart and *The Charlotte Observer* than we were in our mission. We violated ourselves when we got caught up in responding to the criticism of the press. We were constantly justifying this and justifying that. We lost our sight of our mission and developed a mean spirit that was rooted in spiritual pride. It wasn't deep, but it was constant.

When a person loses his sense of mission, he begins doing the same things they are accusing the other person of doing. It's only natural.

Recently, I visited Jim Bakker in prison, and we talked at great length about our reactions to *The Charlotte Observer's* articles and what we should have done instead. We both agreed that we should have listened more and spoken less. We were determined to win the battle against that newspaper, and we lost it all because of our lust for power.

Undiscerned spiritual pride usually requires a serious jolt before we can see it in ourselves.

"But if ye bite and devour one another, take heed that ye be not consumed of one another" (Gal. 5:15).

The Truly Blessed

Some believe that the evidence of God's blessing upon them is the car they drive, the house they live in, their good job, and their riches. To equate riches or material things as a sign of the blessing of the Almighty is to completely misinterpret the message of the Scriptures.

The truly blessed, our Lord says, are those who are blessed by God: "Blessed are the poor in spirit [humble] . . . Blessed are they that mourn . . . Blessed are the meek . . . Blessed are they which do hunger and thirst after righteousness . . . Blessed are the merciful . . . the pure in heart . . . the peacemakers . . . Blessed are they which are persecuted . . . Blessed are ye, when men shall revile you . . . and shall say all manner of evil against you falsely, for my sake" (Matt. 5:3-11).

Tozer wrote in his classic work, *The Pursuit of God:*

In the world of men we find nothing approaching the virtues of which Jesus spoke in the open words of the famous Sermon on the Mount. Instead of poverty of spirit we find the rankest

kind of pride; instead of mourners we find plea-
sure-seekers; instead of meekness, arrogance;
instead of hunger after righteousness we hear men
say, "I am rich and increase with goods and have
need of nothing;" instead of mercy we find cruelty; instead of purity of heart, corrupt imaginings;
instead of peacemakers we find quarrelsome and
resentful; instead of rejoicing in mistreatment we
find them fighting back with every weapon at
their command. This kind of moral stuff civilized
society is composed. The atmosphere is charged
with it; we breathe it with every breath and drink
it with our mother's milk. Culture and education
refine these things slightly, but leave them basi-
cally untouched. A whole world of literature has
been created to justify this kind of life as the only
normal one.[1]

Unfortunately, the attitudes listed by Tozer are not
limited to the world of the ungodly. The same traits seep into
the Church and contaminate everyone they touch.

We are no different than our worldly brothers. Don't
we as Christians often equate recognition, honors, plaques,
and rewards with spirituality? Don't we consider earthly
possessions and human relationships as a sign of God's
favor?

We have missed the mark completely.

Our Saviour did not teach that riches were an indication
of God's blessing. In fact, our Master said it is hard for a rich
man to get saved. In fact, Jesus said, "It is easier for a camel
to go through the eye of a needle than for a rich man to enter
into the kingdom of God" (Matt. 19:24).

Jesus also warned about the "deceitfulness of riches"
because He knew it would always be a problem for the
Church.

Job was a rich man, but he had his priorities in place.

How do we know? Because he said: "Though he [God] slay me, yet will I trust in him" (Job 13:15).

How many "in name only" Christians would curse God if they lost all of their material possessions the way Job did?

Because God loves us, He will remove anything that gets in the way of your relationship to Him. "For whom the Lord loveth he chasteneth, and scourgeth every son whom he receiveth. If ye endure chastening, God dealeth with you as with sons; for what son is he whom the father chasteneth not?" (Heb. 12:6-7).

The way of the Cross leads home — and it is stained with blood.

When we see God as He is; ourselves, as we are; and the vision of duty, we will discipline ourselves to walk a road of humility. That's the truly abundant life. It is the loss of "our" power that truly gives us strength.

Choosing the Lesser Place

In one of his books, Francis Schaeffer introduced me to a word I hadn't heard before. The word is *extrude*. To be extruded is to be forced out under pressure into a desired shape. Francis Schaeffer writes:

> Picture a huge press jamming soft metal at high pressure through a die so that the metal comes out in a certain shape. This is the way of the Christian. He should choose the lesser place until God extrudes him into a position of more responsibility and authority.[2]

Then Dr. Schaeffer suggests two reasons why we ought not to grasp the larger place.

First, we should seek the lowest place because there it is easier to be quiet before the face of the Lord.

We see this happen over and over again, and perhaps it has happened at some time to us. Someone, whom God has been using marvelously in a certain place, takes it upon himself to move into a larger place and loses his quietness with God. Ten years later, he may have a huge organization, but the power is gone.

Schaeffer says the size of the place is not important, but the consecration in that place is.

Second, we should not seek the larger place because it disqualifies us for Christian leadership.

If we deliberately and egotistically lay hold on leadership, wanting the drums to beat and the trumpets to blow, then we are not qualified to serve God or others. Why? Because we have forgotten that we are brothers and sisters in Christ with other Christians.

Schaeffer goes on to say,

> I have said on occasion that there is only one good kind of fighter for Jesus Christ. The man who does not like to fight. The belligerent man is never the one to be belligerent for Jesus, and it is exactly the same with leadership. The Christian leader should be a quiet man of God who is extruded by God's grace into some place of leadership.

We must not be like the little fellow dusting off the boss's chair and saying, "Some day I'll sit in it, and I'll make people jump."

We are servants not lords, stewards not owners. That's a tough lesson to learn; but until we master it, we are not truly free.

Do you seek power or are you a servant? Are you willing to follow or must you lead? Do you quietly listen to your heart or forge ahead with great abandon? Your answers determine the condition of your heart.

A Difficult Decision

For as long as I can remember, I knew God had called me to the ministry. There was a brief time, when, as a young man playing baseball, I considered becoming a professional ball player. But, in my heart, I knew all that I really wanted was to minister to others.

To prepare myself for the ministry, I enrolled at North Central Bible College in Minneapolis, Minnesota, where I received my theological training.

After leaving college, I traveled with my friend, Daniel Johnson. We called ourselves "Dick and Dan" and spent our time singing and preaching our way across the Midwest. For most of the past forty-one years, hardly a week has passed that Dan and I have not talked and shared with one another. He remains, to this day, my dearest friend.

Not long after Dan and I went our separate ways, I married the love of my life, a precious girl, Mildred Nickles. A few months after the wedding, we moved to Chillicothe, Missouri, where I pastored a church for a very short time. But my heart longed to be back on the road, traveling and helping people.

One of our first crusades was held in Watertown, South Dakota. From there, we traveled across the States, ministering wherever we were invited.

When Mildred and I started out together, we were amazed by the acceptance we found. Doors of opportunity opened before us at every turn. Even as a young minister I was invited to speak at large churches and conduct special conferences.

Not long after the birth of our daughter, Deanna, Mildred and I returned to our home area. A sense of security enveloped us as we once again enjoyed the fellowship of friends and family.

During that visit, a church in the neighborhood where I had been raised contacted us. The board explained their progressive vision for the church and offered us the pastorate at a salary almost four times the amount of money I was earning then.

"We'll finally be able to settle down and be near our families," Mildred remarked.

About the same time, however, we received a call from the smaller parish in Watertown, South Dakota — 800 miles from home. Now what do we do? In our hearts, Mildred and I both balked at the idea of living so far north, where long, cold winters and blizzards were common.

It was a difficult decision, but the longer we thought about it we could not escape God's direction. In our hearts, we knew that South Dakota would be the place where God could develop our character. For me there would be fewer opportunities to be in the limelight. I also felt that it could well be a time of testing.

"I believe God wants to set us apart to allow us to come to know Him," I told Mildred. It was for that reason alone that we accepted that assignment.

In the months ahead, however, we often wondered if we had made the right choice.

While pastoring in South Dakota, I was smitten with Crohn's disease, a devastating disorder causing painful inflammation of the digestive tract. I spent several months in the hospital, lost sixty-five pounds, and ultimately had to have about seven feet of my intestines removed. Very few people die with Crohn's disease, and fewer get well. The doctors told me I would have to learn to live with my condition.

When we looked back on that experience, Mildred and I realized that we were in God's will because we deepened our relationship with the parishioners, came to a better knowledge of ourselves, and made a clear commitment to God. In addition, we developed friendships that have become lifelong. We were better people for having been ministers in such a wonderful community that seemed to us to be the lesser place.

The Place of Blessing

After several years in South Dakota, I received a phone call one day from Rev. Rudolph McAdams, the pastor of a church in Garden City, Kansas, a remote town about 50 miles from the Colorado border and 50 miles west of Dodge City, Kansas.

"Our time here is finished, and the church would like you to be their next pastor," he informed me.

Several years before, my wife and I, as young ministers, had conducted a three-week crusade at the Garden City church. During that time the pastor's wife had said to me, "Someday you will be the pastor of this church."

I remembered her statement as I considered the pastor's proposal. These were such good people, and this church had been an influence on my life. Still I didn't want to commit myself.

"I don't think it's the right time for me to come," I told him.

"Then we will wait to leave until it is the right time!" he responded.

In the back of my mind I knew that a church in Kansas City, Missouri, also needed a pastor, and that was where I wanted to go.

To my delight the Kansas City church invited us to meet with their pulpit committee. Afterward, they extended the invitation for us to consider their church.

One night as my wife and I were praying, I realized we were about to make a terrible mistake. I was made to know that I was getting out of the will of God.

Actually, I hadn't really sought the Lord on where He wanted us to go. After all, the larger, more prestigious church in Kansas City seemed the obvious choice. What future would I have at the smaller Garden City congregation out in the middle of nowhere?

That night after prayer, my wife and I said, "Lord, if the church in Garden City calls us again, we will accept their invitation. You know where we are, and You know where they are. If You want us to go, they will call."

About 1:30 a.m. that same night, the phone rang.

Pastor McAdams said, "Pastor Dortch, there are about sixty people at the church praying right now. We are praying that whomever God has chosen to pastor this church, the Holy Spirit will put a fire under them."

My response was, "Go back and tell them to turn off the heat. We are ready to come."

The following Sunday, three days later, we arrived in Garden City, Kansas. That evening the congregation elected me as their pastor, and Mildred and I began one of the most pleasant experiences of our ministry. What appeared to be the back-side of the desert turned out to be an oasis of love, where problems in the church were quickly quelled by praying people. In fact, the congregation in Garden City probably blessed us more than we ever contributed to them.

The lesser place is always the place of blessing.

I have often asked myself if I made the right decision in taking the position at PTL. When I look back now, I still believe that we went there for the right reasons. But I can't help but question my motives.

As a young man, I only sought the kingdom of God and His work. When I accepted the position at PTL, my priorities had changed. At that time in my life, I had immersed myself into my goals and dreams and visions. I was more committed to advancing myself than doing the will of Him who sent me.

I didn't know it at the time, but the grip of fatal conceit had taken hold of me. Within the short span of three years, I was strangled in its clutches — a victim of my own quest for power.

---

[1] A.W. Tozer, *The Pursuit of God* (Camp Hill, PA: Christian Publications, Inc., 1982).
[2] Francis Schaeffer, *No Little People*

15

The Power to Wound

*The arts of power and its minions are the
same in all countries and in all ages. It marks its
victim; denounces it; and excites the public odium
and the public hatred, to conceal its own abuses
and encroachments.*

Henry Clay

What is it about human nature that thrives on the
misfortunes of others? What evil lurks in the heart of a man
that incites ridicule and scorn at the expense of another? And
who can measure the power of words and deeds to diminish
and destroy a person already beset by difficulty and pain?

"Death and life," the Bible declares, "are in the power
of the tongue" (Prov. 18:21).

In his memoir, *Right from the Beginning,* Patrick
Buchanan describes an incident that sadly illustrates this
truth. While Buchanan was an editorial writer for the *St.
Louis Globe-Democrat,* a scandal erupted in the Missouri
Penitentiary in Jefferson City. Warden E.V. Nash bore the
brunt of the criticism and drew the fire of the prestigious

newspaper. Buchanan writes:

> By late 1964, repeated stabbings and bloody racial brawls were calling national attention to the 128-year-old institution in Jefferson City. . . . I wrote editorial after editorial, attacking the prison administration, trying to make prison reform an issue in the gubernatorial campaign. . . .
>
> With the election as governor of Warren Hearnes, who had promised to look into the horrors, action seemed at hand. Nevertheless we kept the pressure up with a final blast in the weekend edition of the *Globe*, on December 15, titled "New Broom for the Prison." In the editorial I took Warden Nash apart — and demanded his dismissal. The paper and editorial hit the streets at 7:00 p.m. Friday and ran the entire weekend. . . .
>
> As nothing else, however, that campaign to clean up the Missouri Penitentiary — taken for good motives and with legitimate cause — brought home to me the awesome power of the press.
>
> The steady hammering of stories and editorials upon Warden E. V. Nash, an uneducated man who had risen from prison guard, was worse for him than any physical beating could have been. We destroyed his professional reputation; and then we destroyed his self esteem. Later, friends would tell me Nash had unknown and grave family problems that troubled him deeply; but it was that same Friday night that we leveled a final volley at him, that he had come home from a Christmas party with his wife, pulled out his revolver, and shot himself to death.[1]

The awesome power of the press! The power of words!

Such Were Some of You

While I was in prison, the inmates would gather around the television to watch the evening news. Many times I cringed as the cameras focused on Christian leaders crying out for longer and tougher sentences for those convicted of crimes.

Imagine my embarrassment as the scowling faces of ministers came on the screen ranting against those whose lifestyles they obviously despised. It was with grief that I saw religious leaders making fun of the homeless and the poor, saying they needed to get a job.

I sat with my friends from the ghettos and the cities of America — bank robbers, drug addicts, businessmen, lawyers, government officeholders, bankers, and law enforcement personnel who had fallen. For the first time, I saw things from their point of view. I wanted to cry as the representatives of God on earth did everything but curse those who carry the heaviest burdens.

Many so-called "druggies" come from the ghetto and don't even know who their mothers and fathers are. Most were abused as children and grew up with no one to care for them. Who are we to add to their load?

Do we represent the Saviour, the One who said, "Come unto me all ye that labor and are heavy laden and I will give you rest?" The One who said, "Love your enemies" and "Love your neighbors as yourself."

Let us come down from our ivory towers and listen to what a very wise Man said, "Let every man be swift to hear, slow to speak, slow to wrath: for the wrath of man worketh not the righteousness of God."

Is it any wonder that so-called "Christians" and the right wing of the Christian community are some of the most despised people in our nation today? Taking hidden cameras into dens of iniquity, they expose the "sinners" on television, screaming about the wickedness of the people they have trapped with their cameras. They have forgotten,

"Such were some of you."

Friend of Sinners

How did God's message through His Son, Jesus Christ, of love, forgiveness, and mercy become so twisted that millions now equate the Christian message with hate, bigotry, and cruelty? You will not find Jesus in a hate-filled mob. He will not be carrying a sign and screaming hatred to already hurting people.

The only time we find Christ in a violent confrontation is not with so-called sinners but with the religious people who have turned the church or temple into a "den of thieves." It was religious people who faulted Christ at every turn. The scribes and Pharisees were constantly trying to trip Jesus.

When Jesus and the disciples were eating dinner at Matthew's house, there were many notorious swindlers there as guests. The Pharisees were indignant. " 'Why does your teacher associate with men like that?' " (Matt. 9:11;LB).

" 'Because people who are well don't need a doctor! It's the sick people who do!' was Jesus' reply. Then he added, '. . . learn the meaning of this verse of Scripture, "It isn't your sacrifices and your gifts I want — I want you to be merciful." For I have come to urge sinners, not the self-righteous, back to God' " (Matt. 9:11-13; LB).

History teaches us that to sit down and eat with someone in Bible times signified a commitment of lifetime fellowship. Our commitment can well be diverted to other things. Sometimes the cause takes second place to our desire for advancement.

Throughout His life, Jesus was reaching out to sinners with compassion. He was even called a "friend of sinners." We never find Him verbally or physically beating up "hurting sinners." Jesus said His Father sent Him into the world to save it, but God did not send Him into the world to condemn it.

Jesus said to the Pharisees, "The Son of Man has come eating and drinking, and you say, Behold, a Man Who is a glutton and a wine drinker, a friend of tax collectors and notorious sinners" (Luke 7:34;AMP).

Jesus had no political agenda to advance His own cause. He was a friend of all — and *especially* sinners.

Cast the First Stone

When the scribes and Pharisees caught the woman in the very act of adultery, they threw her in front of the crowd who had been listening to Jesus' teachings. The law was clear, she was to be killed by stoning.

Jesus did not go by the law, He functioned with grace. And grace superceded law.

How did these religious leaders catch the woman in the very act of adultery? Were they peeking? How did they know about it?

Their big agenda was rules, power, and authority. Many power hungry people are legalists. They know the rules, and they apply them. They call it being consistent.

Thankfully, our Lord was not consistent on this issue. Sadly, there are some who are not like Jesus, and they will not function by grace. They seek to be people of power, lords over others.

Jesus stooped, wrote in the dust, and His finger spelled out a message. It was an act that surely must have put the woman's fears at rest. Why? It was an act of humility. Jesus did not shout at her about her sin. Instead He spoke to her accusers, "He that is without sin among you, let him first cast a stone at her" (John 8:7).

Slowly, they all dropped their weapons and left. Then Jesus said to the woman, "Neither do I condemn thee: go, and sin no more" (John 8:11).

The Pharisees had not been worried about the woman's spiritual condition or how they could help her. Their goal was to be part of the religious "in crowd." They accused her for their own advancement. They didn't care about the woman's life of heartache and abuse. Their purpose in exposing her sin was to make them look good.

Our demands of others often reflect more about us than the sin we are condemning. Much of what we do as Christians is motivated by our fear of what other people think.

Let's not be modern day Pharisees who hurt the hurting and add to the heavy-laden more shame and guilt and despair.

Of No Reputation

Unlike the Pharisees, Jesus, "made himself of no reputation." How many of us can say that about ourselves?

We never find our Saviour hobnobbing with the political and religious leaders of the day or being worried about what was politically correct.

We err gravely when we use political issues as a spiritual test. Our job is not to advance ourselves with a political persuasion, or to increase the funds we raise by these charlatan methods. We must minister to all not just the party faithful.

Do we love a hurting world or do we join in the political action to control those with whom we disagree?

Even the disciples, when they were with Jesus the last time, just before He ascended into heaven, wanted to know if at this time He would restore the Kingdom to Israel. They wanted an earthly kingdom and an earthly throne. The disciples wanted to change the political system, advance themselves, and be a part of an elitist ruling class.

Jesus was only interested in changing people's hearts so that they could change their world. That is why our Saviour simply stated, "It is not for you to know the times or the seasons . . . . But ye shall receive power, after that the Holy Ghost is come upon you: and ye shall be witnesses unto me" (Acts 1:7-8).

After they got more of the Spirit of Christ into their

hearts, their prideful quest to be elevated to political prominence vanished. Once their hearts were transformed, they were able to turn their world upside-down — not with political adventurism but with the message of love and servanthood given to them by the Lamb of God.

Let us listen closely to the words of our Master: "If any man will come after me, let him deny himself, and take up his cross, and follow me" (Matt. 16:24).

Few of us want to pick up the cross or the towel to wash the feet. In our hunger for domination, we aspire to climb the ladder in our religious-political world, only to draw attention to ourselves. When that happens, the true meaning of our faith is lost in our skirmish for advancement.

We must stop the hurting of others and love the world as a loving God does.

Where Were We?

During the fall of PTL, and leading up to the trial of Jim Bakker, the press had a field day at the expense of Bakker and his family. Charlotte radio personalities, John Boy and Billy, engaged in the most ribald and savage mockery of the fallen family. With little regard for truth and none for mercy, the gladiatorial onslaught continued day after day. The mood prevailed in the city of Charlotte and across the nation.

A friend of mine mingled with the crowd the first day of Jim Bakker's trial and later described the circus-like atmosphere at the Federal Court House as an old limousine drove up bearing a couple dressed like Jim and Tammy Faye. When the fake defendant and his wife, accompanied by attorneys, pulled up to the curb, reporters applauded and cheered, "Let the hanging begin!"

Several days later there appeared in *The Charlotte Observer* a significant piece written by psychiatrist Dr. Kevin Denny titled," Jimmy, Where Were We?" The insights he suggests and the questions he raises are profound:

188 • *Fatal Conceit*

I've only met Jim Bakker twice, but it was on the two most difficult days of his life.

The first meeting was by design. His psychiatrist had called me and asked whether I could come to Bakker's attorney's office to provide a second opinion regarding his ability to participate in his own defense, and to arrange for local hospitalization, if needed. I spent an hour with him, while his own psychiatrist and attorney were in court explaining his situation to the judge. Of our meeting I will say little, other than I agree with the court-appointed forensic psychiatrist who diagnosed Mr. Bakker as having a stress reaction with panic attacks.

Our second meeting was by coincidence. I had completed my rounds at one hospital and found myself with a rare commodity, an hour to spare before my next appointment. It was to be the last day of Charlotte's "Trial of the Century" and I decided to drive by the courthouse and witness for myself the media zoo I had heard so much about.

I was initially surprised by the calmness of the courthouse scene, which had been described as chaotic. It wasn't until I had drifted toward the courtroom that I experienced the avalanche of activity that judicial mandate can set in motion. I followed the crowds, passing the bailiff at the door with unexpected ease, and entered to sit among the reporters who filled the visitors benches.

It was soon clear that the court was reconvening simply to obtain additional documentation needed by the jurors, who would provide their final verdict within the hour. Satisfied with the tastes and smells of the trial, I was ready to move on to the rest of my schedule for the day.

But, as the court room was disgorging, Mr. Bakker spotted me — perhaps, I felt, as a strange new face among the battalion of tireless reporters who had spent the last twenty-five days welded to their reserved seats. But then he gave me a hand signal, indicating that he would like to talk to me.

In the cavernous anteroom of the courtroom he approached me — he, surprisingly serene for the circumstances, I with a flush of embarrassment that I had come to the courthouse that day out of curiosity and not compassion. We talked for a moment or two where we had met (within view of reporters eager for each and every novel crumb). I was aware that with a single handshake the anonymity I had been able to preserve from our first meeting had been annihilated.

Mr. Bakker then asked if I could go upstairs to talk with him for a minute or two. My working hypothesis was that under his calm outward appearance the pressure might again be building to the point that he needed a safe outlet for his emotions, so I followed him up to the file room on the second floor that had served as his sanctuary during the trial.

But that was not the case. He was calm and controlled and I was caught off guard by what he did seem to need. He wanted to know if I could talk with him someday about the experience we had shared that day in his lawyer's office. He said it still haunted and terrified him that his mind had snapped, and he felt he was going to need my help to understand what had happened to him.

Mindful that, if the Vietnam experience has taught us anything, it is that trauma experienced easily becomes trauma relived, I told him I thought he was right: Regardless of the outcome of his trial, he would have a whole range of things from the past that he would have to deal with, perhaps requiring therapy and healing over years.

He kept urgently bringing me back to that hour in his attorney's office (yes, with him lying beneath the sofa, his knees tucked to his chin). That was the moment he needed me to help him understand, not all the other things that had led to his trial, but the question, how can a human mind break?

He talked about the terror he felt of not being able to think, to organize thoughts, to relate to others, or to know whether his mind would ever work again.

Then he told me that he had seen the video of himself being escorted by federal marshals from his lawyer's office only the day before. He was amazed at how he looked. Then he asked, quizzically, "But what I really can't understand is where were you people? Where were you people who know what mental suffering is and that the mind can break? Where were all you professionals who could have told people what can happen to the human mind and how terrifying it is when it snaps? Where were you when they made a joke out of mental suffering?"

And I know he was right. Where were we?

I think I know where I was: safely ensconced behind my shield of confidentiality. In my mind, what I had experienced with Jim Bakker that day in his lawyer's office could in no way be distinguished from what every patient can expect to experience with a psychiatrist. What is shared is shared with the understanding that it is confidential. Without confidentiality there is no trust, and without trust there is no therapy. In other words,

Jim Bakker's mental condition was no one else's business, and my responsibility was to keep it that way.

My silence was clearly self-motivated as well. I had no desire to become identified by the media as a person worth pursuing for quotes. Nor did I wish to become known as "Jim Bakker's psychiatrist," for my own well-being and that of my patients.

Thus, I had rationalized that my psychiatric duty had been done when the marshals entered my "office" and carried my patient away in shackles. My professional utility and responsibility had ended. I retreated as quickly as I had entered.

But where was I when radio station WRFX's John Boy and Billy took their morning DJ routine to the steps of the courthouse and made fun of mental illness, encouraging passersby to put their head under their couch for fun and laughs?

Where was I when comedians built their routines around Jim Bakker's mental illness? Or when the cartoonists had their field day? Or when friends made snide remarks, or acquaintances asked me, as a psychiatrist, whether I thought Bakker could be "faking it?" Or when strangers made light of mental anguish?

Where was I?

... Let me start with an offer to John Boy and Billy. Next time you are under stress and experiencing the pains of a mental illness, call me. Perhaps it will be when a loved one dies, or you lose your job, or your marriage disintegrates, or a pediatrician tells you that your child has a terminal illness. Give me a call. I'll do my best to make a mockery of it and fill you with laughs. If that doesn't ease the hurt, we'll set a booth in front of the courthouse where passersby can join us as we giggle our way back into the Dark Ages.

After Dr. Denny wrote this letter, John Boy and Billy, the radio disk jockeys had their day of mockery for him, ridiculing this kind, caring, and gentle man.

Later on, after Jim Bakker went to prison, John Boy had his own run in with the law and was charged in a drug offense. The public was ready, as always, to crucify anyone who makes a mistake, even if it's a popular disk jockey.

Dr. Denny, unlike his less merciful radio personalities, responded with understanding. He wrote another letter to the newspaper asking the public to give John Boy a chance to put his life together.

You and I hold the future of some hurting, weary soul in our hands. We all face situations where we have the opportunity to wound. The power is in our hands. We also have the power to forgive and let healing come. The choice is ours to make.

[1]Patrick Buchanan, *Right from the Beginning* (Boston, MA: Little, Brown, & Co., 1988).

16

The Power That Forgives

Forgiveness is a wonderful thing unless you're asked to do it.

C. S. Lewis

At the end of the Sunday evening service at a Texas church where I was preaching, a well-dressed man came to me. Without many opening remarks, he said, "Pastor Dortch, my wife and I just came from a funeral home. We were paying our last respects to a man who was my best friend for the past twenty-eight years."

I began to offer the usual statements of condolences, but he hardly noticed and continued talking. "He was my business partner as well as my dearest friend. We often talked about how we had built up our business together, and that our unity and faith in Jesus Christ had made it possible. It was true. Everyone around us, including the people who worked for us, knew how we cared for each other and that our families were equally close."

I wondered what to say. Obviously this man was deeply grieving, but something else seemed to be on his mind. His next statements left little doubt.

"Pastor Dortch, about six months ago the worst imaginable thing happened. A very trivial matter came up, and at the time I got ugly about it. I blamed him for the problem, and he reacted pretty much the same way. The entire staff of our company knew about our Christian commitment, so they were naturally shocked. Some were even devastated as the disagreement grew.

"Different people took sides as the word spread. Soon we became arch-enemies. It was a tragedy beyond words, but neither of us admitted any fault in the matter. For six months he and I didn't even look at each other, much less speak. The testimony that both of us had worked so hard to build all those years was destroyed quickly."

He stopped talking for a moment, looked around as if searching for the right words, then continued.

"Last week, broken in spirit, the Lord got hold of my heart. When it was all said and done, I knew I had been the one who had caused the problem. I wrestled and struggled with it, but finally I knew what I had to do. I had to make it right and admit that I was at fault.

"The very next day, I got on the elevator just as it was closing. As the door shut me in from the outside world, I turned around and saw my friend was standing there! We were all alone — for the first time in six months. Without hesitating, I stuck out my hand and said, 'I'm sorry. Will you forgive me?' He didn't take my hand. Instead, he grabbed me with both of his arms, hugged me tight, and cried, 'I'm sorry, too! Can you forgive me?'

As he spoke, the businessman's eyes welled up with tears.

"Pastor Dortch, do you know why I'm telling you this story? As I said earlier, my wife and I just came from the funeral home. My best friend is dead. We lost what could have been the best six months for us as he prepared for his home-going. Sure, we had a few days after we made everything right, but we wasted so much time and hurt so many people before that. We worked so hard to have a Christian testimony among our co-workers, and I'm the one who caused us to throw it all away."

Suddenly he grabbed my arm. "Preacher, please tell as many people as you can about my friend and me. I'm so ashamed. I don't want anyone else to ever fall in this trap. Only hell could be worse!"

Unforgiveness in the Church

One of Satan's most effective tactics in reducing the effectiveness of Christians is to encourage friction, factions, jealousy, back biting, slandering, and just plain bad manners on the part of believers toward other believers.

Not only does unforgiveness divide the body, it destroys the joy, acts as a menacing canker, takes away power in witnessing, and blocks the free flow of the Holy Spirit.

None of us can boast of being guilt-free in this matter, so there is no need for me to point my accusing finger at you (or vice versa). Instead we must recognize this continuing problem as we step under the Lord's searchlight. To work as effective Christians — especially in leadership roles — we must have freedom from the destruction of unforgiveness.

Howard Bushnell wrote, "Forgiveness is man's deepest need and highest achievement."

Charles H. Spurgeon bannered the truth in a more blunt manner. "Forgive and forget," the great preacher said. "When you bury a mad dog, don't leave his tail above the ground!"

But too often the Church, with its many diverse opinions and personalities, becomes a holy court for deciding "right" and "wrong". No one ever agrees, however, and resentment and bitterness are simply clothed in religious garb.

How do we avoid the unforgiveness pitfall? Is it possible? And if we are bound in unforgiveness, what can we do?

Judge Not

The Bible talks more about making things right and having a spirit of forgiveness than it does about heaven or hell! Yet how many times do we feel justified in varying from Christ's plain-spoken words?

He was speaking to His leaders when He taught this truth:

> And when you stand praying, if you hold anything against anyone, forgive him, so that your Father in heaven may forgive you your sins (Mark 11:25;NIV).

Likewise, during His Sermon on the Mount, Jesus revealed the deep hurts caused by unforgiveness — to both parties involved:

> Do not judge and criticize and condemn others, so that you may not be judged and criticized and condemned yourselves.
> For just as you judge and criticize and condemn others, you will be judged and criticized and condemned, and in accordance with the measure you [use to] deal out to others, it will be dealt out again to you.
> Why do you stare from without at the very small particle that is in your brother's eye but do not become aware of and consider the beam of timber that is in your own eye? (Matt. 7:1-3;AMP).

Sometimes, as leaders, we must make careful judgments, especially in the area of discipline. Paul outlines these areas specifically in his letter to the Corinthians, as well as his personal epistles to Timothy and Titus.

> Don't have anything to do with foolish and stupid arguments, because you know they produce quarrels. And the Lord's servant must not quarrel; instead, he must be kind to everyone, able to teach, not resentful. Those who oppose him he must gently instruct, in the hope that God will grant them repentance leading them to a knowledge of the truth (2 Tim. 2:23-25;NIV).

Our problem, too often, is that we feel like others are waiting for our opinions. Opinions — regardless of their religious garb — do not usually lead to unity and forgiveness. Everybody differs, and when the differences arise, truth often flies out our stained glass windows.

You must remember that my name is Dortch. With "sauerkraut" running through my veins, I constantly have a battle with not only wanting to be *right* in every issue but I also want everyone to admit that I'm right (even when I'm wrong)!

Through the years I have discovered how to check whether or not the Holy Spirit or *self* is winning when I am involved in a business-type meeting or confrontation. In the midst of the discussion, I try to examine myself to see how strongly I feel about the point of contention at hand. If I sense that I am trying too hard and feel too adamantly about my point, that's probably the best indication that I'm wrong. Because when I'm wrong, my spirit becomes wrongly directed.

Too often we clash with others simply because we are determined to have our own way. Willfulness and self-assertiveness are many times signs of immaturity and ignorance.

We scheme and connive rather than forgive as we

should. Then, later, we discover that the other person was right! Church history — ancient and recent — is rife with tragic illustrations.

Is it any wonder why the little girl prayed, "Oh, Lord, make more people Christians, and then make more Christians nice!"

"Harmless" Gossip

Petty revenge ever lurks in the wings of a Christian's heart, anxious to assert itself in the guise of righteous indignation — sometimes termed "contending for the faith" or other religious-sounding phrase.

How many of us love to gossip (though we don't actually call it by its real name)? We hear about backsliding or crass sin by a fellow Christian or brother minister and can hardly wait to tell someone else. We always do it because we "need to pray" for them, of course. Invariably, in the telling, the story grows and becomes distorted, usually to the injury of everyone involved.

Then somewhere along the way we fall for Satan's trick of joining the adjective "harmless" to the noun "gossip". What a trap!

Gossip becomes both the seed and the many-faceted harvest. So much would be different if we knew the result of our judgmental words and actions.

A poem written long ago points us to the truth:

> Pray do not find fault with the man that limps
> Or stumbles along the road,
> Unless you have worn the shoes he wears
> Or struggled beneath his load.
>
> There may be tacks in his shoes that hurt,
> Though hidden from view,
> Or the burdens he bears placed on your back
> Might cause you to stumble, too.

Don't sneer at the man who is down today
Unless you have felt the blow
That caused his fall, or felt the pain
That only the fallen know.

You may be strong, but still the blows that
    were his,
If dealt to you in the selfsame way
At the selfsame time —
Might cause you to stagger, too.

Don't be too hard on the man who sins,
Or pelt him with words or a stone,
Unless you are sure, double sure,
That you have not sins of your own.

For you know perhaps if the tempter's voice
Should whisper as soft to you
As it did to him when he went astray,
Twould cause you to falter, too.

                         Author Unknown

God, deliver us from our critical, sniping, super-spiritual attitudes! There must be a better way, if only we would let Him show it to us.

Living in Torment

Recorded in Matthew 18 is the story of the unmerciful servant who owed his king ten thousand talents. The debtor begged for a little more time to pay the bill, and the king granted amnesty.

Soon afterward the same servant accosted one of his own debtors and immediately asked him to pay the hundred pence (a pittance compared to the ten thousand talents). The second servant asked for more time but was flatly refused.

The king, being told by others who were outraged at

what was done, called the wicked servant back in and said these terse words:

> I forgave thee all that debt, because thou desiredst me:
> Shouldest not thou also have had compassion on thy fellowservant, even as I had pity on thee?
> And his lord was wroth, and delivered him to the tormentors, till he should pay all that was due unto him.
> So likewise shall my heavenly Father do also unto you, if ye from your hearts forgive not every one his brother their trespasses (Matt. 18:32-35).

People live in torment because they will not forgive. Without going into details that would embarrass the person involved, let me give a quick example.

I was preaching in a church, and after the service a woman came up to me.

"Pastor Dortch," the lady said, "I have harbored something against you for twenty-eight years, and I want to ask your forgiveness."

Needless to say, I was shocked! I had no idea what she was talking about.

"You probably don't even remember me," she continued, "but when you were just out of Bible college, you used to date my close friend. You had even planned to marry."

It was true. Before Mildred and I knew God had given us to each other, I had been engaged to someone else. Several things happened to help me see that I should marry Mildred, so I had broken off the first relationship. Everything had ended amicably between the other girl, her family, and me.

"I was supposed to be in the wedding party," the woman interrupted my thoughts, "and when you broke off the engagement, I was very hurt for my friend and disappointed about the wedding plans. All these years, I have kept that bitterness locked inside. I've watched you on television and seen your picture in magazines. Each time was a reminder of how hurt I had been."

She once again asked my forgiveness, and I asked hers, but I felt so sad for her as I walked away from that conversation. How tragic that she had carried unforgiveness against me for a quarter-century, and the person she refused to forgive wasn't even aware of her hurt!

Churches, unfortunately, are filled with unforgiving people. We carry grudges against others. We build walls instead of bridges.

I've met people who become so anti-faith movement that they wish Kenneth Hagin would get seriously ill so he could be proven wrong! I've seen others who secretly gloat when any of the prosperity-oriented ministries have financial problems. Can God bless such rabid examples of bitterness and unforgiveness? I cannot believe that the Father enjoys seeing us put each other in walled compartments.

"He who cannot forgive others," George Herbert once wrote, "breaks the bridge over which he must pass himself."

It's Not Easy

The telephone rang. Bob's wife answered, and in five seconds his world ended. He was guilty, and now she knew the secret of his infidelity.

Tears of stunned disbelief streamed from her eyes as he admitted the truth.

Bob asked, "How much do you want to know?"

"Everything," she replied.

For hours they sat in the kitchen and talked. Into the night he gave her explanations, descriptions, confessions. After many tears, they sat in heartbreaking silence. There was nothing else to say.

Then Bob explained what happened next. "She came

over to me, put her arms around my neck, kissed me, and said, 'I want thirty more years.' "

That is forgiveness.

But, you say, it's not easy. No. If it were easy, it wouldn't be forgiveness.

C.S. Lewis wrote, "Forgiveness is a wonderful thing unless you're asked to do it."

As human beings we hold an awesome power over those who have wronged us. We can choose to forgive or we can withhold our forgiveness. The Bible says,

> Do not withhold good from those who de-
> serve it, when it is in your power to act. Do not say
> to your neighbor, "Come back later; I'll give it
> tomorrow" when you now have it with you (Prov.
> 3: 27-28;NIV).

God's Word is remarkably clear concerning the need for pure attitudes. God created us to be forgiving creatures.

Jesus pointed the way to forgiveness, especially through His death on the cross. He did not belong there; the captors had no right to place Him in front of the people in shame; still, He went willingly to His death. He was the King of kings and Lord of lords, but people spat on Him and ridiculed Him.

"Father forgive them," Jesus cried, "for they do not know what they are doing" (Luke 23:34;NIV).

Throughout history, God has been working to bring people into a right relationship with Him, then into right relationships with others. The two are tied together with the cord of forgiveness. God cannot forgive me until I've forgiven others.

If unforgiveness dwells in a person's heart in one relationship, it will dictate the format for all other relationships (whether we realize what is happening or not).

A psychologist who specializes in Christian therapy

recently told me that *most* of the people (who are generally Christians) he counsels have deep-seated problems because they have not forgiven someone.

Through the apostle John's pen, Jesus Christ struck directly at the importance of heart-forgiveness:

> We know that we have passed over out of death into Life by the fact that we love the brethren (our fellow Christians). He who does not love abides (remains, is held and kept continually) in [spiritual] death.
>
> Anyone who hates (abominates, detests) his brother [in Christ] is [at heart] a murderer, and you know that no murderer has eternal life abiding (persevering) within him (1 John 3:14-15;AMP).

Where Forgiveness Begins

Lewis B. Smedes writes in his book, *Forgive and Forget*, "If you are trying to forgive, even if you manage forgiving in fits and starts, if you forgive today, hate again tomorrow and have to forgive again the day after, you are a forgiver."[1]

Most of us are amateurs at forgiveness, bungling duffers sometimes. So what? In this game of life, nobody is an expert. We are all beginners.

Forgiveness begins inside each of us. Even if we can justify building walled fortresses in our homes and in our churches to partition our many grudges and differences, we must forgive before God can use us mightily.

"Sure, Brother Dortch," you say, "it's easy for you. You've been preaching about forgiveness for years. You're easy to get along with. You've probably never faced what I'm facing."

I have been preaching about forgiveness for decades,

and I am trying to be easy to get along with, but this is the truth: God continually deals with me about forgiveness. I get my feelings hurt just like everyone else. Words leave scars on my heart. In my humanness, I have the potential to carry grudges and bitterness. But I have also been around long enough to know that God has a better way.

Recently, I was once again faced with a massive decision on this subject of forgiveness. I would be ashamed to write down what I would have liked to have done to the person who had hurt our family so much. As the day approached for us to meet, I was reminded of the very things that I had taught others through the years.

When the time came, I cringed to hear the sound of his car in our driveway. But as I opened the door to greet him, something happened within me. At that moment, God soaked my spirit with love, and we both knew I had forgiven him.

"He who forgives," an ancient philosopher once said, "ends the quarrel." Forgiveness only comes as we allow God to forgive through us.

Once we move into forgiveness, the Holy Spirit is able to unblock all the dams inside us. Soon we can become open, unclogged channels of blessing to others.

> Little children, let us not love [merely] in theory or in speech but in deed and in truth (in practice and in sincerity).
>
> By this we shall come to know (perceive, recognize, and understand) that we are of the Truth, and can reassure (quiet, conciliate, and pacify) our hearts in His presence (1 John 3:18-19;AMP).

Forgiveness is not an option! If we do not forgive, we will not be forgiven.

The Answer

If unforgiveness is wrong, destructive, sinful displeasing to God, and injurious to relationships, there must be an antidote.

Basic to the question of true forgiveness is the realization of God's love. He loved us first. Jesus Christ did not come to die for haloed saints but for the worst and ugliest sinners.

By example, the definition of a Christ-like love must involve these elements:

> Love is patient, love is kind. It does not envy, it does not boast, it is not proud. It is not rude, it is not self-seeking, it is not easily angered, it keeps no record of wrongs. Love does not delight in evil but rejoices with the truth. It always protects, always trusts, always hopes, always perseveres. Love never fails (1 Cor. 13:4-8;NIV).

The kingdom of God is hindered because so many of us who call ourselves Christians show little evidence of Christian love and forgiveness.

Those in leadership roles must bear some of the shame for Christianity's lack of forgiveness. Through our attitudes and actions, we reproduce what we are. But where love and forgiveness are lived and instilled, by word and deed, the world will beat a path to experience its refreshing and life-giving power.

We place such importance in the Christian world upon human success, but I contend that guarding our spirits against unforgiveness and bitterness should rank much higher on the list of priorities. We burn the bridge to heaven when we do not forgive others. Through bitterness we allow Satan to strip us of our power and wholeness.

Some Christian leaders spend most of their time searching for the sins of everyone else. They try to play God —

always seeking to keep everyone in line with doctrinal interpretations and simultaneously signaling, "I'm doing this because I always know what is best for God's flock!"

When that happens, instead of feeding the sheep with love, truth, and forgiveness, they end up scattering them. Jeremiah addressed that problem among Christian leaders quite bluntly:

> Woe be unto the pastors that destroy and scatter the sheep of my pasture! saith the Lord (Jer. 23:1).

Our God-given place is to love and forgive, then to nurture others to exhibit the same traits.

Dietrich Bonhoeffer in his book, *Life Together,* writes about Christian brothers and sisters forgiving one another in the church:

> And is not what has been given us enough: brothers who will go on living with us through sin and need under the blessings of His grace? Is the divine gift of Christian fellowship anything less than this, any day, even the most difficult and distressing day? Even when sin and misunderstanding burden us in the communal life is not the sinning brother still a brother, with whom I, too, stand under the Word of Christ? Will not his sin be a constant occasion for me to give thanks that both of us may live in the forgiving love of God in Jesus Christ?[2]

As Christian leaders we must rip the rear-view mirrors out of our spiritual vehicles. We must quit looking back at the sins of others. Forgiveness is the best way to start looking ahead.

To Be Forgiven

Christian love must move beyond forgiveness and into the realm of reconciliation.

> Therefore, if you are offering your gift at the altar and there remember that your brother has something against you, leave your gift there in front of the altar. First go and be reconciled to your brother; then come and offer your gift (Matt. 5:23-24;NIV).

God's love is matchless, mighty, sweeping, embracing, forgiving, healing, and cleansing — without reproach, recrimination, or criticism. He is full of compassion. And He expects no less from us.

In Gastonia, North Carolina, a Charlotte suburb, a crowded church graciously received Mildred and me on a spring Sunday evening. The pastor, David Scruggs, gave us the opportunity to tell our story. He really believes in forgiveness, even for a fallen minister like me.

As I spoke, I asked the people to forgive me for the hurt that I had brought them and the hurt that I had brought to their church.

After a time of deep soul searching for all of us, Mildred and I were greeting people as they left the auditorium. When just about everyone had left, one man remained, seemingly waiting for us to speak to him. I approached him and met a young, broken person.

"Do you remember me, Pastor Dortch?"

"No, I'm sorry. I don't."

"I have been a local Charlotte disk jockey, and music producer. Do you remember the song 'Pass the Loot'?"

"Indeed I do." I then remembered the tune that the Charlotte radio stations had played for quite some time. PTL for us was "People That Love." But for some it simply meant "Pass The Loot." It was an offbeat, lively melody.

"I wrote the song and produced it," he said.

I was stunned.

"I am here tonight to ask for yours and Jim Bakker's forgiveness. I'm ashamed that I wrote that song. I realize that now. Please forgive me."

He was trying hard to hold back the tears. I told him to let them loose. I cried, too.

A bitter enemy of ours who had laughed at us and accused us, was now asking to be forgiven. Of course, we forgave him. How could we do anything less?

> Be merciful, just as your Father is merciful. Do not judge, and you will not be judged. Do not condemn, and you will not be condemned. Forgive, and you will be forgiven (Luke 6:36-37;NIV).

The healing balm of love is desperately needed in a world where Satan tempts everyone to nurture resentment, harbor strife, and explode in hateful hurts. We must come to the point where we see ourselves as one with all others who walk this planet. Although, as Christians, we are chosen people, in our hearts we are just exactly like everyone else — sinners in need of forgiveness.

[1]Lewis B. Smedes, *Forgive and Forget* (San Francisco, CA: Harper San Francisco, 1984).

[2]Dietrich Bonhoeffer, *Life Together* (San Francisco, CA: Harper San Francisco, 1992).

17

Dangerous Tendencies

> *We in America are fighting the money power; but if men can elsewhere get the power without money, what do they care about money? Power is what men seek, and any group that gets it will abuse it.*
>
> Lincoln Steffens

One evening I had dinner with a man who had recently been elected to a high church office. Caught up in his new status and position, he had some questions for me.

"How should I act?" he asked. "What role shall I play? What image should I project?"

Since that meeting, I have given much thought to those questions.

It is one thing to have a quest to be effective. We all want to do well and serve faithfully. We want to be useful to our business, church, government, or profession. It is something quite different, however, to want to become something we are not so that we may impress others or hold on to power.

That is the heart of my concern, and it is the root of much evil.

Do you think of Jesus as a religious person? Did Jesus intend that there would be bosses, in the worldly sense, in the church or the world? Why do people in religious work need authority? Why do they seek to lord over people when Jesus simply came to love and to care for us?

God's prime concern is people — not the religious structure. If that is so, how can we justify this lust for power among the religious? What is the motivation behind the desire to assert oneself?

It can be seen in all of us — even in children. "My dad is bigger then your dad. My mom makes more money then your mom. Our house is bigger then your house." It is a part of our nature.

As we mature and become responsible adults, nothing changes, however. When we are placed in a place of responsibility or leadership, our childish, selfish nature rises to the surface. Why does a person's demeanor change when they are elected to an office?

When serving on national boards on different occasions, I would often smile to myself and think, *The people in my hometown church are just as spiritual and smart as these folks. In fact, the folks back home could probably have done the job a lot faster and spent less money doing it than the big shots sitting around the conference tables.*

Adolph Bedsoll, writes in *The Pastor in Profile,* "It is easier to authorize a committee to do a job then it is to arouse and enlist the people to do the job, but people are always better then committees."[1]

The Mob Mentality

Take five good, honest people, elect or appoint them to

a committee, and once the meeting begins the chemistry changes. I have seen it happen over and over again. Loving, kind, caring people enter a room — each with a singular desire to do good — and suddenly, they all bristle like alley cats and the fur starts flying.

Law enforcement officers dread the mob mentality. Something happens to good people when their individuality is swallowed up in a mob. The same herd instinct takes over in board meetings and committees. As individuals the people involved would never have attacked a weaker brother or hurt a friend. Collectively, however, they will take on a mentality that looses its perspective.

How well I remember sitting in various business meetings conducted by religious organizations. I could always tell when people were positioning themselves. Facial expressions, voice levels, and concept of their own worth would change when — together with others — they grabbed for power. Individuals, who would never dream of being malicious or unkind to others on their own, sensed the support of other power-driven people and were suddenly sucked into a web of grandeur.

I used to wonder, *Are these the same people who moments before had bowed their heads in prayer and asked for God's guidance in their meeting?* The mob mentality had taken over their personalities, and God was conveniently forgotten.

Bedsoll writes again, "Messengers or delegations are brought to a point where they are not so much concerned whether you are a Christian or a devil, but they are vitality concerned whether you are 'in or out'."[2]

Once a mindset develops and intentions are declared, factions and cliques begin to emerge. Then more time is spent politicizing to get votes for a particular cause than praying to God for His leadership.

Power drives people; influence leads them. Learn to recognize the difference.

If, as Charles Swindoll suggests, only a few can handle a full cup, why do we gravitate toward the platform and toward position and rank? Why this love affair with recognition and competition? How much better life would be in the home, business, government, or the church if we would develop relationships rather than build fences and empires.

It is tragic to see people who under the influence of an abusive person become hard and mean spirited themselves. That is one of the dangers of submitting to some kinds of authority.

Let's look at the other dangerous tendencies that can lead to the abuse of power. You need to be able to recognize them in others so you can deflect their control before they overpower you. At the same time, you need to look at yourself and see if any of these tendencies are taking root in your life.

A Dominating Spirit

Regimentation to some degree is essential in any business, school, or organization. But when the person making the rules does not permit others to develop as the individuals God created then to be, we need to step back and evaluate the situation.

Even the church can become a big-business enterprise that operates with cold indifference. Our "business" must go on, they say. But where is the caring for the individual within the institution? It is simply: Obey our rules, keep quite, let us put you into our mold.

When a person produces a rigid hierarchy that allows for no change or input and does so in an abrasive manner, it is legitimate to ask, "What is the purpose for all this unbending structure?"

If the demands of a person or organization takes away from your personal relationship with God or your commitment to your spouse and family, then they are asking too much. That's when you need to ask, "Is the regimentation actually a means of controlling others in an effort to maintain power?"

It is a horrible thing to murder independent thinking and to browbeat people for whom Christ died into silence and submission.

"Dogmatic devotion to duty is one thing, dictatorship over a group is another."

Take a look at your own life. Do you seek to dominate people and hold them under your thumb? Do you demand loyalties from them that you would not be willing to give to others?

If so, the yellow light should go on in your mind. There is danger ahead.

Loss of Sensitivity

Getting caught up in a power force can be an intoxicating experience — I know, I have been there. The further away from people we get in decision making, the more likely we are to only think of our own agenda and forget what it is and who it is that we are really dealing with.

One of the dangers of the centralization of power is the loss of sensitivity to the hurts, dreams, and lives of others. The true cause for which we labor is often lost when one or a few seek to rule over all. This is especially true in church denominations, Christian ministries, and other non-profit organizations.

In any enterprise that involves fund-raising, it's easy for the goals to become numbers instead of names. Admittedly, a lot of religious work is big business, and it should be run in a businesslike manner. It is unfortunate, however, when human beings are reduced to paying units and partner numbers.

To the credit union, the bank, the credit card company, the IRS, and the Social Security office you are but a number. To Jesus you are somebody special. He calls you by your name. The power hungry, however, see everyone the same.

When churches or businesses or organizations are in a growth mode, the challenge of keeping sensitive to the needs of the people becomes even more difficult. To save time and money, an aura of "we have to be consistent" takes hold.

That would be okay if every person had precisely the same problem and came from the same set of circumstances. Then consistency would have some measure of legitimacy. I have seldom seen in my work as a leader where any two people were in exactly the same situation and had the same precise set of problems.

Sensitivity and creativity are essential in dealing with people as individuals. Nothing in our official acts as leaders should prevent us from being what we are supposed to be — like Jesus.

Centralization of power often takes advantage of people when they are hurting and downtrodden. When we see that happening, the alarm should go off in our minds.

Sometimes, even in religious organizations, normal courtesies and professional ways of dealing with employees and constituents are lost. When a pompous attitude takes hold of those who are in authority, they are the last ones to notice. Swallowed up in their ivory-tower-leadership, they can't see the forest for the trees.

A Disdain for Change

Institutions, governments, churches, denominations, or businesses that maintain a rigid, top-down, leadership style often loose touch with the man in the pew or the customer at the counter. The layers of leadership and perks isolate leaders. I know because it happened to me. As a result of this isolation, it's easy to become oblivious to the signs of the times.

To make matters worse, those at the top of the heap often have a disdain for change and new ideas. It is not the new concepts that they are afraid of; it is the loss of power.

To change old habits is not easy especially when those in power see themselves as kings. One of the best things that could happen is for leaders to come down from their thrones and submit to a horizontal sharing of leadership.

Sometimes old structures are too ponderous to be effective and operate efficiently. This is especially true of church denominations and Christian organizations. To make necessary changes, we need to continually challenge the premise of what the church should be doing to respond to present needs. We must have a vision and be restless and discontented with the status quo.

The danger of remaining passive could make us extinct. The world used to wait to hear what the Church had to say; no one is waiting now!

Are You a Person of Power?

How can we know the traits, the characteristics, of the person of power? Using common sense and spiritual measurements, you can judge yourself and also gain an understanding of the power people around you.

For people of power, time is not a factor. They are obsessed. They usually will not let up.

A few are more subtle and will stand on the sidelines watching and waiting for the kill so they can attack and pick up the spoils.

The grasp for power — that is their fulfillment in life. Nothing takes its place. It is the journey not just the kill that counts.

They always have a sense of "I have to be right." People who are intoxicated with power cannot imagine or perceive themselves to be wrong. Their insecurity demands a period. No questions asked.

They must be in control; they cannot turn loose.

They must speak to every issue.

They love prominence, position, and power.

They cannot see things as they are, but only as the way

they want them to be.

People of power will walk over, crush, or eliminate by deception anyone who gets in their path.

They would rather be the head than the hand.

Every person who has a place of authority — spouse, parent, leadership role at the work place, officer in an educational institution, government official, overseer or operator of a business, or professional — needs to ask the heart-searching question: Am I a person of power?

Do I seek to be a master or a servant?

Who do I care about most? Myself or others?

In God's kingdom, the person in the place of power is actually the servant of all.

Open Up Your Life

It's difficult to look at ourselves in a transparent way. Why? Because we already have our minds made up.

I must admit I lived in denial for a long time. I could see it in others, but not myself. This couldn't be me the author is writing about, I would think when reading a book. It must be someone else, not me, that the pastor is speaking about.

To get out of our fatal conceit, we must see ourselves and become open about our lives, our attitudes, lifestyles, decisions, and character. To do that, we need to be open in a number of areas.

1. Be open to criticism, good or bad.

If it is valid, learn from it. If it is unjust, don't take the blame for another's ignorance.

The power leader doesn't want to hear bad news, every report has to be positive in order to have a completed circuit. Some leaders, however, don't want a whole picture.

Remember, you are not always right. Your associates may not have the courage to tell you that, but it's true. You do not know it all. Make sure you are submitted to others.

2. Be open to the breath of God blowing from a different direction.

The wind sometimes changes!

Are you open to the creative genius of the Spirit, or are you caught up in our "own" agenda? Are you so stuck on yourself that you cannot see your own blindness?

3. Be open to help, leadership, and direction.

Don't be too stuffy to accept guidance, and don't be too proud to ask for help and prayer. When we become too intoxicated with our own strength, we are often slow to seek help.

Find someone you can trust. If you can't find that person, then you should keep your confidences to yourself.

4. Be open to change!

Realize that the message is sacred, not the method!

Sometimes arrogance needs a full-scale crisis to force change and reality upon us. To change old habits is not easy, especially when we only see ourselves as "kings".

On the other hand, never change simply for change's sake.

5. Be open to relationships.

You will always need fellowship with your peers, your family, and your superiors. You are the loser when you are a loner. Don't burn bridges that you may someday need to cross.

Always include non-Christians as a part of your friendships. You need them. Why? Because they view things from a different perspective and will usually tell you the truth about yourself. Your Christian friends will stroke you, but non-believers will be brutally honest.

6. Be open to be your spiritual self.

You are a living epistle, read of all men, so don't

neglect your spiritual needs while ministering to others. You owe it to yourself to occasionally take a break from the stress and pressures.

Read a book, go for a walk. Be quiet. Listen to your own heart. Loving God is so beautiful, especially if you love Him for who He is, not what He has done for you lately.

7. Be open to denying yourself.

Live a life of self-denial!

"If any man will come after me, let him deny himself, and take up his cross, and follow me" (Matt. 16:24). Few people know or even understand what this means. But this is where many people of power go wrong. They refuse to deny themselves.

To make a deliberate decision to willingly give up positions or assignments that we know or feel are rightfully ours is truly denying ourselves. It's not easy to make a disclaimer to our own wills, but the peace and joy it brings are well worth any discomfort. When we realize that living for self is not enough, we can then reach for a higher and more noble cause.

We must choose to pick up the cross. It is not thrust upon us. Our will must be totally submitted to "His". Lord, Thy will be done, in earth — in me. We were created from the dust of the earth. When God's will is done in earth — in me — His will be done in heaven.

When we make the choice to humble ourselves and live a life of self-denial, we will live for God and for others.

God wants to protect us from ourselves — if we will let Him. If we don't, pride and power will be our downfall.

[1]Adolph Bedsoll, *The Pastor in Profile*
[2]Ibid.

18

Passing the Test

Temptation is the tempter, looking through the keyhole into the room where you are living; sin is your drawing back the bolt and making it possible for him to enter.

J. Wilbur Chapman.

Each of us has had, or will have, our own encounter with the power game. In fact, we have all engaged in the quest for power at one time or another.

But how much power do you have over yourself — over your sinful nature? Can you pass the test and possess your own spirit? How are you at governing your own life?

The test we all face is temptation. We don't talk about it much, but it is ever before us.

Henry Ward Beecher, the renowned clergyman said, "Find out what your temptations are, and you will find out largely what you are yourself."

When we come to know ourselves, then we can pinpoint our weaknesses and be on our guard against our particular temptations.

The great preacher J. Wilbur Chapman said, "Temptation is the tempter, looking through the keyhole into the room where you are living; sin is your drawing back the bolt and making it possible for him to enter."

Maybe you've jokingly said this oft-repeated phrase, "I can resist anything but temptation!" Do you feel the only way to handle temptation successfully is to yield to it?

None of us is above falling. It is a fact of life, "All have sinned, and come short of the glory of God" (Rom. 3:23).

"If we say that we have no sin, we deceive ourselves, and the truth is not in us" (1 John 1:8).

We have all succumbed — at one time or another — to the temptation to gain power or exercise the power we have over other people. That doesn't mean, however, we can't learn to be victorious the next time.

The Temptations We Face

The lie that Satan told Adam and Eve, "Go ahead and do it. It won't matter," is the same lie being used today.

Let's look at three kinds of temptations that every Christian must face and how we can learn to resist them.

1. The test of our devotion to God.

Man of destiny, Abraham, righteous as he was, was severely tried. God put Abraham to the test. Why? Because Abraham needed to discover the extent of his own consecration and the power of his affections.

Told to sacrifice his son, "thine only son, Isaac, whom thou lovest" (Gen. 22:2), Abraham set out to obey God — whatever the cost.

Before God, angels, devils, and man, Abraham demonstrated his supreme attachment to the Almighty. Then God said, "Now I know!"

Of course, God knew Abraham all along. So, then, what was the purpose of the test? To give Abraham a glimpse into his own heart. He realized he really was a man of faith.

This is the kind of test which, sooner or later, comes to all of us. We will all endure a test of our character and our devotion to God so that we may come to know ourselves better.

2. Temptations that spring out of our own weakness.

Temptation is the pull of a man's own evil thoughts and wishes. These evil thoughts lead to evil actions, and afterward to the death penalty from God.

> And remember, when someone wants to do wrong it is never God who is tempting him, for God never wants to do wrong and never tempts anyone else to do it. Temptation is the pull of man's own evil thoughts and wishes. These evil thoughts lead to evil actions and afterwards to the death penalty from God. So don't be misled, dear brothers (James 1:13-16;LB).

James writes that men are tempted when they are led away by their own lust and passions. When passion gets the upper hand in the imagination, it will become sin and end in death.

When we become stagnant and matter of fact in our relationship with God, we are headed for big trouble. It is a spiritual fact, closely related to the physical law of motion, "for every action there is an equal and opposite reaction." In the weakness of our flesh, we are tempted and led away in our own lust.

That's what happened to King David.

David stayed at home to relax when he should have been on the field of battle. When we kick back and let down our guard, we make ourselves vulnerable to temptation and disaster.

It was C.H. Spurgeon, the master pulpiteer from Great

Britain, who said, "Some temptations come to the industrious, but all temptations attack the idle."

David was tempted to commit adultery when he lingered on the balcony watching Bathsheba. He didn't pass the test, and, as a result, paid a terrible price.

The prophet Nathan pronounced David's judgment for his sin. Let's look at some of the consequences: public exposure of the king's sins; death of the child being carried by Bathsheba; murder of one of David's sons by another; betrayal by his friends; deserted by his own people.

What a price to pay for one night with a married woman!

By contrast, Joseph, as a slave in Egypt, raised the right question when enticed to adultery by his master's wife: "How can I sin against God?"

David didn't ask that question of himself at the time, but he later agreed that "against thee and thee only have I sinned" (Ps. 51:4). By then, however, it was too late to undo the damage done to his family, his nation, and his reputation.

3. Satanic Temptation.
Other tests come after great spiritual victories.

Certain tests and temptations are directed specifically by the enemy of our souls and reserved for more spiritually mature Christians who will not succumb to everyday sins. Satan derives great pleasure from attacking and destroying those who are in the heat of the battle for men's souls and fighting for victory in God's kingdom.

When Adam and Eve were in the Garden of Eden, Satan himself came and tempted them because he knew how important this couple was to God's design for this earth. Since that time, Satan, the deceiver, has periodically tempted men and women whom God had anointed for special tasks. His appearance comes, not so much in physical form but in their minds and imaginations.

Jesus' temptation came after a glorious spiritual experience. At His baptism in the Jordan River, God spoke audibly to His Son and filled Him with the Holy Spirit. In response to the voice of the Lord, the heavens opened. What an incredible manifestation!

Any time the voice of God speaks, look out! There is danger ahead when we believe we have been given a special revelation from God. The temptation is to become spiritually proud. If we fail to handle the situation properly or try to draw attention to ourselves instead of the Lord, we are headed for trouble.

I know from experience that the testing will usually come in our greatest moments of blessing. When things are going well and everything seems wonderful, then beware of the severe attack.

After this incredible demonstration of hearing God's voice and the heaven's opening, a dove came to rest on the shoulder of our Lord. Immediately, however, Jesus "was led of the Spirit into the wilderness."

This is precisely where God wants to take us at times. Why? Because in the dry places, He can prepare and equip us to be used more fully in the future.

Many people fail to realize that they need to fortify their hearts against such attacks. Immediately following any great divine experience, you will certainly come under an attack in your life. I guarantee it!

The attack may come in the form of greater temptations — more money, more prestige, a compromise here, a slip of the tongue there. Appearing innocent and more like blessings than the enemy's curse, the temptations lure you into their trap.

Satan has determined to overthrow us. He knows that any person who is filled with God's Spirit will become an antagonist, a hindrance to his purposes. That's why our hearts must always be right. We cannot risk letting down our guard.

Why the Wilderness?

Our Saviour was led into the wilderness by the Holy Spirit. If you and I use natural intelligence in these matters, we could question, "Why would the Spirit lead anyone into the wilderness?"

When a person is filled with the Holy Spirit, it is for service. First, it is to *be* something for God. Secondly, it is to *do* something for God and others. God doesn't bless us with spiritual gifts so we can have a new way to exalt ourselves or that we may be lifted up. They are given for His glory.

We must never conclude that this service will begin immediately without any real trials. When God intends to use us, we need not jump at the chance immediately. There may be times when we need to deal with our own hearts. That is why we will be tested.

Perhaps Jesus did not know why He was being led into the wilderness. He was very much the man Christ Jesus, and He had a nature like ours in the matter of temptation. His deity did not sustain Him or enlighten Him in this area. For He "was in all points tempted like as we are, yet without sin" (Heb. 4:15)

It is my opinion that Jesus was tempted most of all in the realm of His imagination. Satan came to Him in His thoughts — in His mind. I believe that Jesus was tormented and tortured in His imagination, just as we can be.

In our testing times, many things come to our minds at the suggestion of Satan. Should I take what doesn't belong to me? Why not be unfaithful to my spouse? The thought to cheat, lie, be unfaithful, be jealous, speak against others — everything any human is capable of doing — will come to mind.

In this dreadful and horrible wilderness, Jesus was constantly bombarded by the harshness of the environment, the loneliness, the weariness, the hunger, and the thirst. Even wild beasts attacked Him. Surely, He was tempted to let fear overcome Him.

Sometimes fear is worse than the temptation because the enemy sends fear to confuse, distract, surprise, and wear us down. Jesus was worn down — as we often are — in this mysterious and prolonged test of His spirit, His character, and His life.

The most destructive of temptations and tests come in the desert places of our lives.

The Danger of Loneliness

Jesus was tempted while He was alone. Loneliness can be the prelude to disaster if we don't learn how to deal with it.

People often tell me that in the middle of all of their activities, whether it is among their associates, at home, or even around a lot of people, they feel very much alone.

Loneliness sets up some of the worst temptations. When we are alone, we are tempted to do things we would never do if someone else were with us. I've had people tell me they gave in to temptation just so they wouldn't be lonely.

We must creatively come to grips with what loneliness is and learn to master it.

Loneliness, by itself, is a wilderness. It affects each of us differently. Sometimes no one can help us because our situation is so personal and deep. In some circumstances, our companions, those whom we love the most, do not understand and cannot give assistance. We're on our own. No one is there to hold our hand.

In times of temptation, most of us seek some place of refuge. We want another human with us to share our difficulties. To win the battle and pass the test, however, we must seek victory in the wilderness within our own heart and on our own turf.

Even if you could find someone who understood, it might be to your detriment. Others cannot know what God is trying to do inside you, or they may not care. That's why

you must be careful with whom you share your problems. If
you confide in the wrong person, you could easily end up
with a bigger dilemma than loneliness.

Your greatest temptations and your highest victories
— both seldom take place in public. Temptations, especially, happen behind the scenes, out in the wilderness —
alone with God. But in your loneliness is also where you'll
experience the greatest victories.

Do Something for Yourself!

"If you are the Son of God, tell these stones to become
bread" (Matt. 4:3;NIV), Satan taunted Jesus.

"If you are the Son of God then use your powers to look
after yourself. You are great! You have the power! Show
God's power! Work it! Look out for number one!"

Our enemy was saying to our Lord, "Do something for
yourself!"

How different this was to Christ's teaching: "Whosoever will save his life shall lose it; but whosoever shall lose
his life . . . the gospel's, the same shall save it" (Mark 8:35).

Jesus never performed a miracle solely for His own
benefit. He never promoted His own reputation or His own
ministry. How unlike us. With anything that we do in life, in
business, education, the arts, the sciences, whatever we do,
we want to shout it from the housetops.

Those who use God's power for their own selfish
advantage, however, become trapped in selfishness and
deceit. The final outcome can only be disaster and destruction.

Jesus responded to the devil by using the Word of God:
"Man shall not live on bread alone, but on every word that
comes from the mouth of God" (Deut. 8:3;NIV). Those
words — the sword of the Spirit — became a potent weapon.
With one flick of the blade, Jesus was able to slash Satan's
first temptation to shreds. Our Lord passed the test because
He knew what His weapon was and how to use it.

That's how we will pass our tests — by speaking the
Word of God. What we have in our hearts and in our minds
will be our defense, and God has promised to bring it to our
remembrance. That is why we must commit to memory the
words our Lord said and did. At the time of crisis, the
Almighty will come to our assistance.

Prove Yourself

Our enemy doesn't slink away easily, however. He
pounds; he comes back again and again.

Satan's next trick was to suggest, "Jump off the pinnacle of the temple!"

"If you are the Son of God ... throw yourself down. For
it is written: 'He will command his angels concerning you
...' "(Matt. 4:6;NIV).

Actually, Satan misquoted Psalm 91:11-12. Satan obviously knows the Scripture, but he has no qualms about
twisting the words or "smoke screening" them with half-
truths.

As the Son of God, Christ could have done anything;
He had the authority. Satan, however, wanted to test Christ
by putting Him into an area of presumptuous activity.

Never fall for that. God offers protection and safety,
but His promises are not to be misused, and they are never
to tempt God.

While I was the pastor of a church, a sixteen-year-old
girl, grief-stricken over her uncle's tragic death, came to me
at the funeral home and said, "My great moment has come.
During the funeral service, I am going to lay hands on my
uncle in the coffin and bring him back to life."

Earlier, I had stood with the funeral director and
witnessed the embalming of her uncle.

As lovingly and kindly as possible, I said to her, "You
won't be able to resurrect your uncle because the life of the
flesh is in the blood, and your uncle's blood has been
removed."

God gives us better sense than to test His power with childish acts. He wants us to grow up and get on with important things in the Kingdom and not stay at the place of our temptation.

The temptation to use supernatural power to prove ourselves to others has shot through the minds of many a man and woman of God. Do not at any time listen to such a satanic suggestion.

Jesus answered, once again, with the Word, "Thou shalt not tempt the Lord thy God" (Deut. 6:16). That rebuke simply declares: don't put yourself into situations where you provoke God.

Just This Once!

We are always tempted with the lead-in phrase, "Just this once." That's the big trick. Just do it once. Bow down to me for a moment. Go ahead; no one will know the difference.

Satan's final temptation required that Christ surrender himself. First it was the enemy's mission to ask our Lord to save himself, then show himself, then it was surrender himself. Everything rested on the presumption that the surrender to Satan would only be temporary.

Satan's highest purpose is to get you temporarily out of God's plan for your life — to surrender "just this once" to him, to do just one selfish desire.

That one trick fits so well with the attitude today that says, "I'm answerable to no one." "I'll do as I please." "My wife doesn't satisfy me." "My husband doesn't understand me." And so it goes.

A time will come when you will doubt whether or not you have any connection to the Almighty. There will be moments when you feel that you have no knowledge of God. It can be chipped away, and your faith will come into question. At that point, victory or defeat lies within you.

In your tests, never surrender a righteous position that

you know is right, no matter how many authorities and experts disagree with you. Do not surrender your will, even in the wilderness. Never yield a fraction in your emotions, imagination, or your will. Whatever happens, do not give in to temptation whether it be in the flesh, from the devil, or a combination of both.

If you are governed by your feelings, look out! You are in for serious trouble. Once the enemy gets an inroad into your personality, it will certainly lead into defeat.

Satan was saying to our Lord, "Here's a real clincher. I will save You from the agony of the cross. You can have the world, but You don't need the cross! I will give all power to You."

Never forget it — Satan does have power. Certain kingdoms of this world are controlled by satanic forces. He is the prince of the power of the air.

His offer to Jesus was a big one. "What a deal — for just one bent knee I'll give it all to you, Jesus."

Satan's persuasive arguments always come cloaked in confusion and mixed motives. The issue is never written in distinct black and white.

Jesus knew that it would all belong to Him on the other side of the cross, but what a price to pay. Satan made the temptation very appealing: "Just bow down . . . we'll work together in harmony."

Jesus didn't fall for Satan's lie and refused to submit himself even for a second. Once again Jesus used the Word of God, "Thou shalt worship the Lord thy God, and him only shalt thou serve" (Deut. 6:13).

We must never demand a miracle to free us from our tests or when we are in trouble. God has given us His Word for the test. We must know and apply it and then move forward.

We must say, as the three Hebrew children did to the king, "Our God whom we serve is able to deliver us from the burning fiery furnace . . . But if not . . . we will not serve thy gods, nor worship the golden image" (Dan. 3:17-18).

God is certainly able to deliver us out of any test and trial, but whatever happens, we must submit to His will. We cannot order God around.

The River of Iniquity

Like Jesus, we must overcome the areas where Satan would tempt us. We must conquer:

the wilderness,
the loneliness,
the darkness,
the trial,
the environment,
the weariness, and
the hunger.

What have we learned about dealing with temptation? Let me make a few points:

1. We must resist temptation on our own and only with God's help.

Others can help, but we must be strong within ourselves. We must do it, even when we are all alone.

2. We must be willing to make bold decisions during tests, no matter how confused the circumstances.

Joseph didn't say, "Let me think about it." He didn't say, "I want to talk this over with somebody else." He didn't look for someone else to blame in case the decision caused discomfort. He emphatically said, "I cannot sin against God. How can I bring dishonor upon my master, he trusts me in everything I do!"

3. When we yield to temptation, however temporary, a river of inequity is set loose.

One of the most pleasant and wonderful trips my wife and I have taken was to the Hawaiian Islands. The fauna, the flora, the majesty and beauty of Hawaii must be experienced — it is impossible to describe.

During our visit, a friend took me to a dormant volcanic mountain. I could easily see where the eruptions had sent molten lava down the side. Everything in its way — houses, beautiful flowers, and all signs of life — had been destroyed. There was nothing but hardened rock-like lava.

When we yield to temptation, molten lava begins to pour from our lives, and no one can stop it. A river of inequity is set loose — one that even God will not stop. It is like molten fire — it burns and destroys everything in its path as it runs.

To Soar Again

We are in the hands of a loving, caring God who will always forgive us, even when we fail the test. Nothing we will ever do can stop God from loving us.

When we are tempted, our heavenly Father knows about it. He is touched with the feelings of our hurts and the wounds of our life. Our Lord was tempted in all points as we are. In the proper time and place, He will give us the answers we need.

For Jesus, when the temptation was over, He was victorious. Our Lord had remained pure and faithful and had not yielded an inch to the enemy. Then we are told very simply one of the most beautiful phrases in the Scriptures: "angels came and ministered unto Him" (Matt. 4:11). They gave Him supernatural blessings and power.

The angels gave Him bread from heaven. What a difference. It was the Father's bread, not Satan's temporary, illusionary puff of smoke.

The battle was won in the wilderness. The matter was settled there, and the cross finished it for eternity.

> When you were dead in your sins and in the uncircumcision of your sinful nature, God made

you alive with Christ. He forgave us all our sins,
having canceled the written code, with its regula-
tions, that was against us and that stood opposed
to us; he took it away, nailing it to the cross. And
having disarmed the powers and authorities, he
made a public spectacle of them, triumphing over
them by the cross (Col. 2:13-15;NIV).

The battle in the wilderness was private. The battle on
the cross, however, was a public spectacle! Our Saviour won
both!

Temptation comes to destroy us, to disgrace us, to
bring dreadful harm to others. There is no such thing as "just
this once," or "no one will ever know." It will always
dishonor us when we don't pass the test.

God will see us through as we wait upon Him. "There
hath no temptation taken you but such as is common to man:
but God is faithful, who will not suffer you to be tempted
above that ye are able; but will with the temptation also
make a way to escape, that ye may be able to bear it" (1 Cor.
10:13).

President John Quincy Adams once said, "Every temptation is an opportunity of our getting nearer to God." To
realize God's presence is the one sovereign remedy against
temptation.

You can pass the test. The Word of God works in every
situation and time of testing. And the rewards are well worth
it!

To my knowledge the author of the following poem is
unknown, but it provides a beautiful illustration for those of
us who have not always passed the tests.

As I walked through the woodland meadows
Where sweetly the thrushes sing,
I found on a bed of mosses
A bird with a broken wing.

I healed his hurt each morning
And he sang the sweet refrain,
But the bird with the broken pinion
Never soared as high again.

A young life by sin is smitten
With all its seductive art,
And moved with Christ-like pity
I took him to my heart.
He lived with noble purpose,
He struggled not in vain,
But the bird with the broken pinion
Never soared as high again.

One of my fellow inmates read that poem, and in his grief at having not passed the test, knew of God's love and God's forgiveness. He acknowledged that a bird with a broken pinion could never soar as high again, but he realized that God's forgiveness was complete. So this broken man added a concluding verse:

The life that sin has smitten
With all of its guilt and its stain,
By the grace and merit of Jesus
CAN soar as high again!

19

Total Release

The worst thing that could happen to a person is to be successful before they are ready.
Dr. Martin Lloyd-Jones

About a year ago, a young man walked into my office at the Life Challenge, a crisis agency. He didn't say hello or introduce himself, he just asked, "What's prison like?"

Before I could answer, he continued, "I've gotten involved in some serious legal problems, and I may have to go to prison."

As we began to discuss his needs, he explained how he had gotten to this point in his life.

"One Sunday, my pastor preached a sermon called, 'God Does Not Wink at Sin.' Afterward I tried to fool myself and justify my actions. I knew what I had been doing was wrong, but the combination of fear and pride wouldn't allow me do anything about it. I was trapped with nowhere to turn."

I didn't ask any questions but let him continue to talk.

"I've attended church all my life and was saved as a

young boy. When I was twelve, I started delivering newspapers. Over the next ten years, I built my paper route from one hundred customers to over seven hundred."

He smiled for a moment, then continued. "At fourteen, I attended a Saturday night youth rally. For the first time in my life, I saw kids on fire for Jesus. They loved the Lord and truly loved one another. That night God got hold of my life. Through my high school years, I took over one hundred kids to those Saturday night rallies. Many of my friends were saved. You may not believe this, but I've never had a drop of alcohol or put a cigarette to my lips. I've never even seen illegal drugs."

As he talked, it seemed impossible that this clean-cut young man could actually be facing a prison term. I didn't interrupt since he obviously had come to bear his heart and share his burden with me.

"At that time, God planted a seed in my heart to work with young people. Even after I got married and started my own business, I continued to serve as a high school Sunday school teacher and worked closely with the youth pastor of our church. I had attended college for a year but quit to work as a furniture salesman. At age nineteen, I began building a house. I moved in, then sold it, and started another house. One home a year grew to two, two to four, four to twenty-five, then fifty, until I peaked at three hundred homes in one year."

Finally, I had a chance to break in. "Did you continue working with the youth?" I asked.

"Yes. About this time, the youth pastor position at our church became vacant. This job had been filled by a full-time pastor for over ten years. I didn't know how I'd find the time to do it, but I strongly felt the Lord was calling me to take the position. Because I had never attended Bible college, I felt very unworthy. After meeting with our pastor and the elders of our church, I began serving as youth pastor, which for me was a dream come true. Although I had accomplished much as an entrepreneur, nothing compared to the joy of ministering to young people."

"What about your construction business?" I questioned.

"Along the way, I had started to develop property to have enough lots to keep building houses. My company grew to over fifty employees, and I became the local Wonder Boy. Articles often appeared in the local newspaper explaining how I had become a millionaire at the age of twenty-five. The pinnacle of my success came when I completed a championship golf course surrounded by fabulous homes and condominiums. What thrilled me most was meeting the athletes and celebrities who came to play at my course. It was another dream come true."

As he turned to look out the window of my office, I asked, "How were you able to handle all this sudden success at such a young age?"

"Not very well," he answered, focusing his eyes on my face. "I started to believe my own press releases. I thought I could do no wrong and that every piece of property I touched would turn to gold. I figured I could handle it all . . . alone."

"You mean you felt like you didn't need God anymore," I stated.

"When I started out, everything I did in business I tried to do for the Lord," he said in an effort to explain. "I built quality homes, took care of customers, and tried to treat everyone fairly. I had a good reputation that I was proud of. Probably too proud. I liked being a big shot. The money didn't matter that much to me. Even though I didn't spend it on expensive cars and things like that, I liked the feeling of knowing I could if I wanted to. I really wasn't into power over people as much as the perks that come with money and the power it brings."

"Did you realize what was happening?"

"No. It came into my life so slowly I couldn't see it, and I wasn't accountable to anyone."

"Why was that?" I asked.

"Because if I had to be accountable to someone, then I wouldn't totally be the boss. I wouldn't be everything the newspapers said I was. It would mean I needed other people and that I wasn't smart enough to handle things myself. I guess that's what set me up for the trap Satan had laid."

The look of utter remorse on his face made me want to reach out and embrace this young man, but I knew he had more to tell me before he was ready for ministry.

"My business started to experience cash flow problems. I was working a hundred hours a week, trying to keep things going, but it just kept getting worse. That's when I started making some illegal transactions to raise cash. I knew it was wrong, but I had no idea where it would lead or how severe the consequences would be. Besides, I told myself, it's only this once or only for a week. But once led to twice, twice to four times, one week to two, two weeks to four, and on and on."

He stopped and looked at me for my reaction. "Go on," I encouraged him.

"Once I stepped into the trap, I couldn't get out. Or, my pride wouldn't let me get out. I worked as hard as I could, night and day. I did everything in my power to keep up a false front. When my illegal transactions were eventually uncovered, I knew I had to hire an attorney. I finally realized God does not wink at sin."

"Where do things stand now?" I asked.

"I've pleaded guilty and am now waiting for the judge to decide my fate." He stopped for a moment to steady himself. "I could be facing a prison term," he said, blinking back the tears. "That's why I've come to you, Mr. Dortch."

This time I did get up from my desk and walk around and firmly embrace my new friend. For several moments, we wept together. Me, for what I knew he was facing. He, for the shame and remorse of having failed God.

The Restoration Process

That was the first of many meetings with this young man whom I'll call Mike. At our next appointment, he shared with me what had happened since we last met.

"I can see now that from the moment I was caught, God began His restoration process," he told me. "Although the process isn't always the easy way, I know it's the right way."

I nodded, and he continued.

"God humbled me, broke me, and then started to rebuild me, piece by piece — His way and not mine. I knew I had to go back and confess my sin and ask forgiveness of all those whom I had hurt by my actions. It was the hardest thing I've ever done in my life, but it was part of God's plan and He gave me the strength to get through it. I went to everyone who would meet with me — bankers, subcontractors, customers, investors, pastors. I publicly addressed my church and the youth group to ask their forgiveness."

"What about your family?" I asked.

"My wife has loved and supported me — my mom and dad, too. My pastor and elders have prayed with me on a regular basis. The youth group and their parents showered us with love and encouragement. In fact, the entire church has expressed what true Christianity is all about — love and forgiveness. Even most of my close, personal friends have stuck by me. They've called and made me and my family know we are loved."

"How's your new Christian advisory board working out?" I asked, knowing that three other men had come together shortly after Mike's first meeting with me to advise him on legal and business matters.

"Great!" he exclaimed. "We've been meeting every two weeks. They've really helped me do the right things and make the right decisions. God must have hand-picked these guys because they have been a great blessing and influence on my life. They have become the accountability I needed. I thank God for them."

"What about your spiritual life?"

"I have seen so many miracles in the past few months!" he exclaimed. "God has helped me restore many broken relationships. Although I go through times when I still struggle with the uncertainty of the future, most days are filled with the peace of God. People have actually commented that they can't believe how peaceful I am considering I could be going to prison."

"That's wonderful, Mike," I commented. "I can see a big difference in you from the first time we met."

He smiled. "I realize now that going to prison for a few years is nothing compared to living for many years in a spiritual prison of sin and not being in a right relationship with God. My short term future may be uncertain, but my long-term future has never been more secure."

"Do you have any plans?" I asked.

"My heart's desire is to work with young people again. I can't wait!"

Seven Steps to Total Release

I've shared Mike's story with you for only one reason: in hopes it will keep you from falling into the same trap of fatal conceit. Trying to be something you are not and playing roles that bring no fulfillment puts you in terrible bondage. I know because I lived under the weight of that burden. It is difficult to keep up the act and live a false life everywhere you go — at the home, at the work place, at school, in business, and at church. But you can be free to be yourself.

In order to avoid the pitfalls that Satan sets for every one of us, I want to show you some ways to gain freedom from the deception of power that becomes every man's trap and every woman's dilemma.

Here are seven steps to finding total release.

1. Let loose of any position that controls you.
Decision determines destiny. Be willing to step aside

from any dominate force in your life. If what you do and the position you hold controls your mind, your will, and your aspirations, look out! You are on the verge of being trapped in your own quest for power. When your position means more to you than your focus on God and it takes preeminence over your spouse or your family, you could be headed for tragedy.

The love of position and the belief that you and the job you do are one entity, can have a dreadful effect upon your life. When you only see yourself and the position you hold through the eyes of your title or your claim of recognition, you have sacrificed who you are for the role you are trying to play.

No position, no job, no recognition, or claim to fame should ever control us. You must seek and choose a place of service and only through servanthood and living for others can you find the contentment and "great gain" that brings the peace that you seek.

2. Determine to conduct yourself as a servant.

It's hard to be a servant when everyone is applauding and telling you how great you are. Without question, pride sets up your downfall.

Have a livable lifestyle in which you will never need to be ashamed. Never equate your relationship to others by earthly possessions.

Have a servant's heart that does not seek to be lord over people.

Determine who you are by how much of yourself you have given to others — not by material possessions, the size of your assets, but by your willingness to be spent for others. Jesus calls us to deny ourselves and take up our cross and follow Him.

3. Submit yourself to a friend who will always tell you the truth about yourself.

The wounds of a friend are greater than the praise of an enemy.

When we are intoxicated with power, or we lose a spirit of humility, we can easily spin off in a direction that could be dreadful to us. That is why each of us should develop and maintain relationships of submission to people who love us enough to tell us the truth — all the time and in all circumstances — even when it hurts.

Most of us mentally acknowledge that we need this kind of accountability. When someone attempts to carry out their responsibility of challenging us, however, we may balk at their correction and resent their intrusion.

Only in submitting to others can we find a place of safety. There is something in our nature that tends to get out of line, that seeks to be puffed up, and believes that we are no longer vulnerable. We need to hear this refrain over and over again: submit yourself. That is a place of safety.

4. Give attention to what really matters.

Your relationship to God — that is what really matters most. Not your relationship to working for God and others, but your personal, intimate relationship with the Almighty. Nothing matters more.

Only you know what is going on in your heart. How strong is your commitment to having a living and loving relationship with your Lord?

Your relationship to your spouse. If you are married, nothing is more important than working hard at maintaining that relationship. Your spouse should be the number one love of your life. You should seek not only to please God but to please the one person you love the most.

It's easy to fall into the trap of busying ourselves with religious activity and doing things for others while the person who most deserves our attention sits on the sidelines.

God would never call you to work that would lessen the love, the focus, and the attention you should give to your spouse.

The neglected spouse of a religious workaholic often has no interest in church and is repulsed by spiritual matters. As a result, their marriage dissolves in disunity and eventually divorce. Why? Because the "spiritual" companion cared more for position in the church and the honor of men than caring for their own spouse.

Your relationship to your children. Don't be so committed to a place of service to others that your family ultimately suffers in the end. Before long, your children will be gone, and you will wonder, *Why did I spend all that time on the things that really didn't make that much difference?*

Use your time wisely now to be a loving influence on your children. Don't lust for positions of power — even within the body of Christ — that pull you away from those who need you the most.

Keep fit physically, emotionally, and spiritually. Maintain good lifestyle habits and keep a clear conscious. This is the only way to live. Take care of your body, your spirit, and your soul.

Your relationship to your place of employment. This is the last place of emphasis, and for good reason. Why? Because it often becomes the number one guiding force of our lives. Of course, you have to earn a living and give a full day's work to your employer, but it is not the most important area of your life. When money and your job becomes the central focus, you can become trapped by the success syndrome.

When addressing a business or religious group, I will sometimes hand out pieces of paper that simply say, "Please write down the completion of this sentence: I am . . . ."

Most people put down, "I am a businessman. I am an engineer. I am a professional. I am a minister." In fact, they are persons — they are husbands and wives and fathers and mothers.

You usually think of what you do as who you are, but that is not the way God sees you. If you keep your true identity in proper perspective, you'll focus on the things that really matter and not get off track.

5. Determine to maintain integrity of spirit and conduct in accepting any position of trust.

Even when we are serving others, it's crucial to set some rules and checkpoints for ourselves. If you don't, the time will come when you'll pay any price and do as you please.

Some people can only see the thrill, the honor, and the accolades of their position. As a result, they often lose their integrity in their actions and in their spirit. Why? Because they were willing to do anything to keep up the act and be the leader. Their grip of arrogance became so tight they thought their hold would last forever. But pride brought them down.

6. Be willing to step aside in a place of leadership to prefer another and for the greater good.

During the four years that I was sitting on the sidelines away from ministry, I discovered that God could get along without me.

You, too, will do well to learn that God does not need our approval to proceed with His work. Maybe someone can do the job better than you!

It never occurs to most of us that other people could do our job just as well. In fact, they may even have a greater burden and sense of urgency. But we refuse to budge because we love the glory and honor of leadership.

Many times — in business, government, education, and the church — progress suffers and the work begins to flatten out or go down because a leader cannot relate to what is happening around him. He only sees himself — and never anyone else — in the director's chair with his name blazoned in bright letters.

Be willing to honestly evaluate yourself by asking: "Would I be willing to step aside and give up the place of recognition to another?"

7. Make sure you are ready for any assumption of a position of power.

Let the job or the task seek you out. Be cautious about seeking power yourself. If it is earned and you are ready for it, power can be a beautiful thing. When it happens, however, be sure you have the emotional and spiritual maturity to handle the authority given to you.

I have noticed in my work, both as an administrator in business matters and in leadership among Christians, that most conflicts and failures result from immaturity or irresponsibility. When a person is not prepared for the job given to them, upheaval and chaos follow because ignorance often breeds pride. Unquestionably, the religious scandals and the financial failures of business leaders stem from too much too soon for those too young or inexperienced.

The prodigal son had a right to everything he demanded from his father; it was not wrong for him to ask for what was rightfully his. The problem was he was not ready for the responsibility of handling a large sum of money.

Your worst enemy can be yourself if you seek to acquire and grab for power before God is ready to hand it over to you. Dr. Martin Lloyd-Jones, the world renown biblical expositor of Westminster Chapel in London, England, said, "The worst thing that could happen to a person is to be successful before they are ready."

You're Going to Prison

In the days before I was to be incarcerated in federal prison, the idea of leaving my wife, and our family, overwhelmed me. Pounding in my mind constantly was the thought, *You're going to prison!*

The consciousness of what the future held became

abundantly clear. I was going to prison, I had no choice, I couldn't evade it — I had to go! It hit me with such certainty, and it hit me hard.

That is the day I will never forget. No experience in my life has been as dramatic. I have never known such remorse, such grief, and such pain as I experienced on that momentous day. Many wounds had not yet healed, and the thought of separation from my family ripped me apart.

I asked myself over and over: *How could I have been so stupid? Why couldn't I see what was really happening at PTL before it was too late?* The shame tore at me. Now there was nothing I could do to change the situation.

The thought kept coming back: *I will be in prison in a few days. Like it or not, I am on my way.* It was as if I were being sucked down into a whirlpool and there was nothing I could reach out and grab onto. It was, for me, the most foreboding journey I had ever taken.

The torment wouldn't quit; it continued throughout the entire day.

I was no stranger to physical pain, having suffered for years from intestinal disorders and having passed kidney stones. But this pain was totally different.

That day I died to myself.

When I look back upon my life and all the things that have happened to me, it will be the suffering, the hurt, the pain that I cherish the most. It isn't the blessings, the accolades, or the awards that I will remember — it will be the suffering. Why? Because in suffering we become totally one with our Redeemer.

"I'm Free!"

Only those who have experienced bondage can know what true freedom means. Many Christians don't understand what it means to be free. I have an appreciation of freedom that I could never have known before I went to prison.

I will never forget that first day of freedom after I was released from incarceration. Although I was still in a half-way house in St. Petersburg, Florida, I was permitted, for the first time in over a year, to leave for an entire day. I could go where I wanted to go and do want I wanted to do. The choices would be mine.

When Mildred pulled up in front of the facility exactly at nine o'clock in the morning, joy overwhelmed me. We had lost just about everything we owned, and the only car we had was a well-worn, old Mercury Cougar with about a hundred thousand miles on it. That day it looked like a limousine to me.

When the car stopped, I quickly ran outside and, like a child, jumped into the front seat. I looked across at the one whom I love the most — my dear wife who had stood by my side. Suddenly a sense of total release swept over me. I began to weep, and through my tears, I raised my hands and I looked at her and shouted, "I'm free! I'm free!"

The next thing I shouted revealed the true meaning of my freedom: "There is nothing else to come out. There is nothing left to fear, I am free!"

It was more than my release from the confines of prison that brought me to such heights of ecstasy. It was knowing I had told the truth and paid the full price for my deeds. There were no secrets lurking in the shadows waiting for some reporter or government prosecutor or religious organization to sniff out. I was free to get on with my life and live without the bondage of past sins and failures. I was free to be myself in Christ.

Going to prison brought me face to face with reality. While I was incarcerated, I learned a lot about myself. In that shame and humiliation, I determined never again to allow a proud look, a haughty spirit, or a lust for power or material gain govern my life.

Today, I am free.

Although the experience was painful, I can truthfully

say I am not disappointed that it happened. Why? I am the better because of it. I now know who I am and where my strengths and weaknesses lie.

How do we get to that place where we really know the peace, joy, and contentment that true freedom brings? It only comes when we totally release ourselves and begin to live for others. It comes when we completely submit ourselves to God and to others. It comes when we choose to take the lesser place and follow the path of humility.

20

The Letter

*He giveth power to the faint; and to them that
have no might he increaseth strength. Even the
youths shall faint and be weary, and the young
men shall utterly fall: But they that wait upon the
Lord shall renew their strength; they shall mount
up with wings as eagles; they shall run, and not be
weary; and they shall walk, and not faint.*

Isaiah 40:29-31

In the summer of 1986, I received a telephone call from
a man whom I have always believed is one of the few
prophetic figures of our time — David Wilkerson. In fact, I
considered him, as I do now, to be more than just a "man of
God." I believed he was a principled person who would not
compromise his values. He was not for sale at any cost.

His telephone call caught me by surprise. After a few
brief pleasantries, in a genuinely straightforward fashion, he
quickly addressed the issues on his heart.

He said, "Brother Dortch, I have been seeking God's
face and praying. In listening to the voice of the Lord, God

has spoken to me. I have a word from the Lord. God will destroy PTL. The spirit of the Lord has departed. You should call a solemn assembly to warn the people."

"It's not my ministry," I explained. "I'm not the head of this ministry."

"I know that. When I was in prayer, the Lord told me to call you, Brother Dortch," he said solemnly. "*You* must do something, and it must be done quickly. What is going on at PTL is an abomination to God, and it must be stopped. Brother Dortch, you are the hope of getting some of these problems solved."

In a stunned manner, I responded and explained, "You may well be right, but we need to hear it from you. I am certainly open to the possibility of your coming and sharing with our entire staff your vision."

Without responding to my invitation, he continued, "If something isn't done quickly God is going to write *ICHABOD* over the doors of Heritage USA. The birds are going to be flying in that hotel within a year — unless something is done and there is true repentance."

I implored him to come, but he said it would be impossible at this time. I pleaded with him to meet with Jim Bakker and/or me. He encouraged me to address the staff myself.

"Won't you please come and tell us what you feel? Would you meet with Jim and me?" I begged, my tone becoming more and more insistent.

At the time David Wilkerson called, Jim Bakker was in California. I did my best to get Brother David to come and unburden his soul to us, but he felt that he could not do it.

Warnings

I called a meeting of the entire staff for the next Friday afternoon at 2:30 p.m. Everyone was to be released from their jobs and assemble at the PTL television studio.

By that Friday Jim Bakker had returned from California, and I shared with him David Wilkerson's prophetic word. I told him about the scheduled meeting and asked him to introduce me that day before I spoke. I wanted the staff to know that Jim Bakker was standing with me in what I had to say. Jim cheerfully responded and said he would be glad to do so.

I addressed the staff that Friday afternoon in a way I had never done before at Heritage USA. I dealt with every known sin that I felt God leading me to address, including infidelity in marriage, adultery, homosexuality, drinking, pornography, conversation, and language. I discussed the importance of paying our tithes and living a life pleasing to God. I felt it was necessary to cover the fundamentals of Christian living and the conduct expected of believers.

"Our partners and viewers have a right to expect every one of us to have proper moral values in harmony with our Christian witness," I told the PTL staff. "They have a right to expect us to live an overcoming life — a life above reproach."

At the conclusion of my message, a holy silence hovered over the auditorium.

Upon returning to the dressing room, Jim remarked to me, "If there's anything you missed today, I don't know what it was. And it all needed to be said."

In my soul I felt that I had delivered the message that, in a sense, had been laid upon someone else's heart. But it was a message I knew I had to communicate.

I then called David Wilkerson and pleaded with him once again to meet with us. He reluctantly consented to meet with Jim Bakker and me on the following Thursday in Chattanooga or Knoxville, Tennessee. The next morning, however, his secretary called to say he would be unable to come. I was extremely disappointed.

Other Christians were also sending warnings to PTL. Some of them, without fanfare, privately attempted to lay a foundation on which to get Jim Bakker's attention. They were unsuccessful.

As the year progressed the rumors, stories, and allegations concerning Jim Bakker and a woman continued. I found myself frequently trying to answer the questions that were coming, never imagining the whole matter would explode in our faces.

God Loves! God Forgives!

After ten months of incarceration in federal prison, my health began to fail. At first the prison doctors were treating me for a hernia. During an examination before the surgery, one of the doctors asked, "Why are your ankles so swollen?"

I said, "I don't know."

"We need to do a CAT scan," he stated.

Three days after the hernia surgery, they did the scan and the same doctor came back to my bedside to report the results. "You know, I'm almost positive that you have cancer," he said as gently as possible. "Tomorrow I want to send you downtown and get an MRI."

The next day after the MRI, he told me, "I'm very sorry, but you do have cancer. It's life threatening, and we'll have to remove your kidney."

A few days later, I was back in surgery.

Had it not been for Dr. Rossi, the chief medical officer at the prison, I am sure that I would not be alive today. He and the United States Air Force doctors saved my life. I am convinced that had I not been incarcerated, I would never have taken the time to have had the examination that resulted in my life being spared.

After the operation, recovery came slowly, and I used a cane the last few months in prison and five months after my release.

Even in the Florida heat, while walking out in the prison yard, I wore an overcoat because I was always cold. It seemed I was getting well, but my body hadn't been notified.

One day, a few months before I knew I would be released from prison, I was talking with another inmate, Ed Taylor, a true brother in Christ. "Ed," I said, "I've got to write David Wilkerson and tell him I am sorry."

"Why?" he asked.

"I've got to make things right. When I had begged him to come to PTL, we didn't have an argument, but I could sense there was tension between us. I knew he could not find a release in his own spirit to come to PTL, but I kept insisting. I realize now that I had a contentious spirit. My pleading and urging were not being responded to, and I was used to having my way. I want to be forgiven for my attitude that day when he called and warned me about the pending judgment coming upon PTL."

Ed looked at me for a moment, then said, "Yes, it would be good for you to write to him and clear the air."

Five days passed, and I had not yet written to Brother David. When I went to mail call that day, the officer called my name and handed me a letter.

When I looked at the return address, I read: Rev. David Wilkerson, Christ Church, Times Square, New York City.

My heart nearly stopped, and I thought, *Has he heard from the Lord again? Oh, Lord, I don't need this. Not here; not now.*

Too afraid to open the envelope in the mail room, I went back to my dormitory. It was time for the evening meal. As 163 men filed out to go to eat, I stayed alone in my modular cube.

I sat on my cot, staring at the envelope in my hand. I had already been removed from my denomination. It was my fault, not theirs. Prison had been easy compared to being rejected by my brothers and sisters in Christ. In my weakened condition, I felt I couldn't bear up under more rejection.

In the 22 inches from the side of the wall to the bed, I got down on my knees and began to pray. "Lord, you have helped me to walk through everything that has happened, and so far I've been able to maintain a kind, gentle spirit. Lord, I don't want to allow bitterness into my heart. I want to come through this submitted to You and without any rebellion. So, Lord, when I open this letter and read whatever this prophet of God has to say, help me to accept it with the right spirit."

I stood up and opened the letter.

The first words I read were, "Brother Dortch, I love you."

I sighed, overwhelmed with a sense of relief. I sensed the love he was showing as the love of Christ. The joy, the peace, and the exhilaration of knowing that somebody cared about me flooded my soul.

Then I read that he believed he had a word for me. By then, the fear had lifted, and I knew God was going to speak.

I continued reading. Brother David said he knew when I got out of prison that I was going to try to make up to God for what had taken place. He said he knew I was sorry and that I wanted to do what was right.

I smiled to myself, realizing God knew the inner secrets of my heart.

"I know that you want to do everything you can to make up to God for what took place. Don't try to make it up to God; He wants to make it up to you."

"He wants to make it up to you!" I could hard believe my eyes.

I read on, "There's one thing I want you to know. We have a loving, Heavenly Father."

I came apart; I wept. There was a loving, forgiving Saviour. I knew it! I had preached it for years, but now someone was whispering it to me, "We have a loving Heavenly Father."

God had forgiven me for my pride, my arrogance, my haughty spirit, and now He wanted to do something beautiful in my life. As far as the east is from the west, so far has

He removed our transgressions from us. I realized there is nothing we can ever do to stop God from loving us.

Maybe you're thinking, "Pastor Dortch, I've done things, I've brought hurt to my family. I'm ashamed of myself. I got sucked into the power trap. I've sinned against God. I'm so sorry."

Let me tell you from someone who's been there and back: God loves! God forgives!

I know now what it means when I quote the verse that says, "There is therefore now no condemnation to them which are in Christ Jesus, who walk not after the flesh, but after the Spirit" (Rom. 8:1).

There is no condemnation! I am free, and you can find that release, too.

When repentance and truth merge, a dynamic comes into play, and God begins to open doors for us. When we truly repent and give ourselves in humility to a loving Heavenly Father, we don't need to make anything up to Him. When we submit ourselves to God and to others, we find the true freedom from the trap — this fatal conceit.

Fatal Conceit
is also available in audio for $12.95,
and hard cover for $14.95.

Index

Losing
It All
&
Finding
Yourself

HOW TO
PICK UP THE
PIECES AND
START ANEW

Richard W. Dortch

Richard Dortch knows what it means to lose it all. Fired from his job, forced out of his home, dismissed from his denomination, and facing an eight-year prison sentence for his involvement at PTL, he hit rock bottom. He lost his integrity, his reputation, his freedom, and his sense of self-respect. Standing among the ruins of his life, Richard Dortch dusted himself off and began his journey back.

Only someone who has been there and back can take you up on the mountains and into the valleys and point out the way. With remarkable insight, Richard Dortch shares the secrets of his heart and gives you a glimpse into his soul. You'll come away marveling at the grace of a loving Heavenly Father, and strengthened in your own spirit to face whatever life may bring. And, hopefully, you too will look deep within and find something you may have lost along the way — yourself.

$5.95 • paperback

The fall of PTL cost him two years of his life . . . what went wrong?

INTEGRITY

How I Lost It, and My Journey Back

From its former president, an inside look at the PTL crisis.

Richard Dortch

INTEGRITY . . . it is a potent entity and it has the power to control, change, and alter circumstances along life's perilous path. It is an awesome tool and responsibility. It is an easy thing to lose when taken for granted.

Richard Dortch, former PTL president, candidly discusses what really happened behind the cameras at PTL — how he has faced his own problems, coped with the criticism and condemnation, admitted his own guilt, and asked to be forgiven by God and man.

$16.95 • hard cover — $9.95 • paperback

Available at bookstores nationwide or call 1-800-643-9535 for ordering information

Dear Pastor Dortch,

I want to know more about Life Challenge.

I need help. Fatal conceit has trapped me.
I will be calling you.

I would like someone to contact me for
spiritual counseling.

NAME _____

STREET _____

CITY, STATE, ZIP _____

PHONE _____

LIFE CHALLENGE
Office Hours 9 a.m. — 4 p.m., EST
Phone (813) 799-5433

(Fold here — staple and mail)

stamp

Life Challenge
P.O. Box 15009
Clearwater, FL 34629